First published in the United States of America, April 2013
by Desert Springs Publishing
78-365 Highway 111, Suite 340, La Quinta, CA 92253
www.desertspringspublishing.com
760-219-7008

Photography used by permission
Stock Images licensed by www.iStockphoto.com and www.Veer.com

Andrea Rae Rosenblatt
Post Office Box 10249, Palm Desert, CA 92211
www.entertainingyourway.com
andreaeyw@gmail.com
760-799-3334

Design by Thomas Granade
Edited by Robin Jones

Library of Congress Control Number on file with publisher.

ISBN 978-1-62407-338-0

Printed in China

For my mother, Florence, who taught me to give back,

For my father, Harold, who taught me patience,

For my brother, Steven, who taught me to laugh.

Shalom and Welcome.

One of my joys in life is throwing parties for friends and family, and I've been doing it for more than 40 years. I've planned and hosted countless dinners, birthdays, holiday get-togethers, luncheons, even company picnics and fund-raisers. Over the years, I've learned how to make every party great. My friends consider me the party maven.

Entertaining Your Way is my way of guiding you through the process of planning a party and making it easier than ever. Any get-together — from a casual, spontaneous barbecue to a formal dinner party – should be fun for both guests and hosts. It should never be stressful for anyone.

Still, a lot of people find entertaining intimidating. I'm here to tell you: Don't. The best times with friends, old and new, are unpretentious and relaxed. Getting together to kibbitz is what counts, not how elaborate the decorations are, or how fancy the food is.

That being said, no party happens without some kind of strategy. The key is to be organized. A party begins well before the first guest is invited. It starts with the imagining of a good time — the people, the setting, the food and the conversation. Then you can start to plan, with that image in mind.

And so shalom, and welcome to my world. In these pages, I'll show you what I've learned in my decades of being a hostess. I'll also share with you some words of wisdom from my culture that help me remember that entertaining is not about impressing people, it's about being a mensch and making them feel comfortable and at home.

Simple. Classic. Parties.

entertaining your way

chapter one

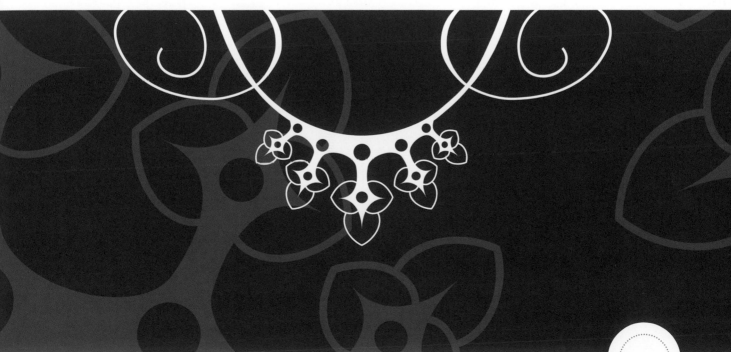

So you're determined to have a dinner party. Perhaps you would like to celebrate something like a birthday or anniversary. Maybe you just saw a fabulous recipe in your favorite food magazine. Or maybe it's as simple as you wanting to have a small group of friends over to have a delicious meal.

Great idea – dinner parties are a great way to have a small gathering. They are also a wonderful way to introduce new friends to old friends. But if you are not organized, they can be quite the source of stress, and a headache. Please know that it is possible to host a dinner party that's fun, controllable and most important, stress free. It's really no secret that the way to have an enjoyable event for everyone, including you, is to take everything one step at a time. The key to any kind of party is to stay organized. Here are my eight time tested steps for planning a dinner party.

dinner parties

< Photo courtesy of Lisa Smiley Photography, Sacramento, CA

> Step 1 : Why have a party?

When planning any kind of party, no matter how big your guest list is, it all begins with a simple question: *Why should we get together, and are we celebrating something?* If you keep birthdays and anniversaries on your calendar, you will always know when someone's birthday or anniversary is, as well as any special occasions. These dates become your window of opportunity for you to throw a party that's appropriate for the event. Times such as these are made even more special when they are celebrated with family and friends. Of course a delicious meal beautifully prepared doesn't hurt. The next time opportunity knocks, turn that into an event in someone's life. They will remember the day with fond memories, as you will. And after all, fond memories is what life is all about.

Although the "why" of the party may seem obvious, it's still important to kick into organization gear. Get out your pad of note paper and start writing, and your planning has formally begun. I keep a separate stack of pink pads for my party planning. That way, everyone knows they are off-limits for everything else.

Your next step should be to set the date. As you review your calendar, it's not only a good idea to check the best date for your party, but also the days and hours surrounding your choices. If you, or a lot of your perspective guests, work from Monday to Friday, a Saturday evening may be the way to go, so you have a day to get ready and you and your guests have a day to recover before everyone goes back to the normal routine. Three-day weekends, are ideal for daytime parties. However, if it turns out that a weeknight is your best choice, keep things simple and casual. Try to pick food that can be made in advance, served easily and especially easy to clean up.

> Step 2 : How do you want to make it different?

Next, decide whether you would like to have a particular style or theme for your party. What's your vision? It could range from something dressy and formal all the way to low-key and casual. When making this decision, think about how much space you have, what your budget is, how many guests you expect and what time you plan to host the party. If you are mindful of these things, your party will succeed.

It's important to remember is that you don't need a big or fancy space to have a dinner party. From a formal dining room to a breakfast area in the kitchen to a small outside patio, any place can work for entertaining. Be creative and organized and you'll have the kind of results you'll be proud of. The best part of this is to do what you want, do what works for you.

CASUAL ENTERTAINING is about creating an ambience of ease and relaxation that flows through the gathering. If you have a dining area in your kitchen, a small dinner party at the kitchen table is always special. It certainly feels cozier than in a large dining room. Picture it (as Mom from the "Golden Girls" television show would say): the chicken is ready to come out of the oven, and there's a freshly baked chocolate cake on the counter. On top of all that, you won't have to leave the room to go into the kitchen and miss any of the fun. When possible, a round or oval table should be used. It helps to create the best environment for people to really talk; no one is at an end struggling to hear what's going on. Low candles are always appropriate for the table; some people say they represent the traditional fire in the hearth. You can add a small vase of flowers, but make sure you have plenty of room for the food platters.

Finally, try to prepare entrées that can be made ahead of time and served family-style. Last-minute cooking and plating should be kept to a minimum; a lot of hustle and bustle in the kitchen may make it harder for your guests to relax. If you choose to set your table in another room, like the dining room or the living room, the seating arrangements and table settings should be simple and inviting, and your menu should be creative but not over the top. In this situation, both buffet and family-style service will work well. Both of these service methods will give you the opportunity to mingle more and spend less time in the kitchen.

FORMAL ENTERTAINING is perfect for a special holiday like Thanksgiving or Christmas or an anniversary. The dining table is traditionally covered with a beautiful white or off-white tablecloth, set with your best dishes, flatware and stemware. Your menu will typically be more sophisticated than at an informal dinner. You can either plate the food in the kitchen or set out a beautiful buffet.

No matter whether the party is casual or formal, prepare a seating chart ahead of time and use place cards in your table setting to guide your guests.

> Step 3 : The Guest List and Invitations

Chances are when you think about planning a party, you already have some ideas about who you want to invite. I keep a master party/social guest list all year round. As we meet new people, I put them on the list. It's just like an address book. When we want to have a party, my first step is to refer to the list.

If you don't have something like that, then your first step should be to start a list. If it's a small gathering, consider everyone's personalities and how they would play off each other. If it's a large gathering, then it doesn't matter as much.

If you have decided on the date and considered your area for entertaining, then you should be able to figure out how many people you can invite. Keep in mind that just because someone said they would come, that doesn't mean that they will. Sometimes there are last-minute issues like work, an emergency or a health problem. It's not unusual to add a couple more people to your list just in case. My feeling is there is always room for two more people somewhere.

There is no set rule on the method of inviting people. We live in different times and we have choices; we can communicate through emails, house phones, cell phones, text messages (not in the car) and the old-fashioned mailed invitation. For a more formal party, or if there's a lot of information to be shared, the mailed invitation is still the best.

The traditional mailed invitation does not have to be costly. It can be as big or small as you want. You can even send a little note on a blank card or nice piece of stationery. Be as creative or as simple as you want, but make sure to include an RSVP date, along with your phone number and email address. If you don't hear from some of your guests, follow up with them a week before the party.

You will need a head count to plan your shopping and seating.

Simple. Classic. Parties.

> Step 4 : Planning the Menu

You know why you're having the party, what your theme is, and how many people you've invited. Now it's time to turn your attention to the menu. This process may seem a little intimidating at first, especially if you are a novice in the kitchen. But don't let it scare you. The more you cook and entertain, the easier it gets.

As you think about what recipes you would like to prepare, ask yourself a few questions: Is this for a special occasion? Are there any food restrictions because of the season? And what can I realistically pull off? As you look through your cookbooks or magazines, make sure you pick out dishes that work well together. You don't want your guests' taste buds fighting each other. Not everything you serve has to be a main attraction. Moreover, your entrée doesn't have to be the big deal in the menu. If you have a specialty dish that is a vegetable or starch, make that your star.

The occasion sets the mood for your evening. Decide whether you're having a formal meal, which customarily means fancy dishes and fancier food, or a casual meal, which normally means a simpler and more fun menu. Also, think about any special ingredients you would like to use that tie into your occasion while you look for recipes. Remember that you can almost always adjust some of the quantities and ingredients.

The season will probably be the most important consideration dictating what you serve. Figuring out what's in season can take away a good portion of the guesswork for your menu. I do start by looking at cookbooks, but I never make any final decisions until I go to my local supermarket or farmers' market. It's a great way to get inspiration as you walk around and see what's fresh. Don't forget to take notes as you see things and taste things. Another consideration might be the weather you're having at the time. If it's cold, snowy or rainy, perhaps a thick, creamy soup would be good. Or is it hot and muggy? Try a cold soup or a cold pasta salad.

At this point, you'll also want to think about your budget, how good you are in the kitchen, how much time you really have to prepare, and whether your kitchen has any drawbacks for throwing a dinner party. These possible challenges do not have to cause you any problems as long as you face them up front and plan accordingly. Do whatever you need to do in order to accomplish what you want. Think about serving an entrée that can be made ahead of time. Or, if you have a lot of limitations, make your dinner a potluck and let your guests participate.

It's perfectly appropriate to buy any part of your meal if you don't have time to prepare everything. You have endless choices for the first course, whether you go to a regular market, a specialty market, a deli, or a deli section. Even take-out pizza or barbecued ribs can work for an entrée, especially if you serve them with a big tossed salad and a scrumptious dessert. And of course your dessert choices are numerous.

After you have given thought to the above questions, it's time to review the balance of your menu. Is the first course rich or smooth and creamy? Add a dessert that has fruit in it. On the other side of the coin, is the dessert rich? Then start with a light salad. If the main course has a kick to it, complement it by starting with a fresh salad and ending with something creamy. Feel like being different? Don't serve the traditional meal consisting of a meat, starch and vegetable. Rather, set out your vegetable as your first course. That could be a cold salad or a hot vegetable.

Now it's time for the artist in you to come out and consider how your plates look. Will your dinner plate have any color? If not, try adjusting your menu to have some potatoes mixed with a small amount of green vegetables, or even just a splash of dill, so you can liven everything up. Also, a lot of times soups and desserts are pretty plain. If you have them, now is the time to bring out your colorful plates.

By all means, do not forget the bread. To many, bread is a main course, and at minimum a side dish. Fortunately, it comes in an assortment of many textures, sizes and shapes. A bread basket is a must-have. Fill it with a little of everything, and don't forget the butter.

Now that the menu is set, the next thing to figure out is how you are going to serve it. Use what you have, or you can borrow. If you want to buy serving plates or dishes, you can get different kinds pottery, copper or brass. About 90 percent of what I have is white, because it goes with everything and all foods. My personal philosophy on platters is this: I want the food to make the statement. I would rather someone say the food looks delicious, rather than complimenting the platter. Another thing to consider is how you want to garnish your dishes. This is another side of presentation, and the details are everything. I suggest garnishing your dish with an ingredient that represents what's in your dish. Not only does it look pretty, it also gives your guests an idea of what they're eating. For example, if you're serving a chicken piccata with a lemon, butter and caper sauce, slice a few lemon wedges and place them on the chicken. If you're serving rosemary potatoes, gently place a couple of fresh sprigs across the top.

Finally, decide which beverages you would like to serve. Do you want to offer your guests a full bar? Or just beer and wine? The basics for a home bar are always bottled water, nonalcoholic drinks, beer and wine. Not everyone wants to go the full bar route, as it can be very costly, especially if you don't normally keep a lot of alcohol on hand. If you do want to have a full bar, just set up a little self-serve station off to the side. I think it's fun to have a signature cocktail for the party. During one Memorial Day weekend, I threw a luau-themed party. Our signature drink was called "Shipwreck," and we served it in a plastic Tiki cup. We then let everyone take their cups home. That's the kind of detail your guests won't soon forget.

> Step 5 : Serving Styles

Once your menu is set, the next step is deciding how to serve it —

RESTAURANT-STYLE means that dishes are individually plated in the kitchen. This is appropriate for more formal occasions, and is also a good idea if your table is small and cannot accommodate the amount of platters you're using. For a little variety, consider serving dessert and coffee in another room like your living room or outside patio if the weather permits.

FAMILY-STYLE works well for informal occasions. The food is arranged on large platters and placed in the center of the table, where guests serve themselves. If a platter is large or heavy, the guests can help each other while they each help themselves, or the host can always walk around the table.

BUFFET means that you arrange your food on a table that is usually covered with a simple tablecloth. Guests can help themselves. This works well for both formal and informal meals. It is especially effective for larger groups because it not only allows people to eat in areas other than the dining room, but it also gives them more opportunities to mingle. It's important to allow some traditional seating for guests who are more comfortable eating at a table, especially if they have health issues. Also, you do not need to offer all of the food in one place. Providing multiple food stations will help avoid traffic jams and, once again, will encourage guests to mingle.

Simple. Classic. Parties.

> Step 6 : Take Care of Details

Seating, regardless of the kind of party you are having, is best pre-planned. You certainly don't want to be schlepping chairs across the room and over your guest's feet. Use whatever chairs you have or can borrow as long as they look good together. As an alternative, if your budget allows, you can always buy slipcovers. Should you discover that the chairs you have are not conducive for extended sitting, think about adding some cushions. If all else fails, you can always rent.

Next, you must make a seating plan. Assigned seating is not just an old-fashioned tradition. It's also an effective tool to put your guests at ease when it's time to eat. Plus, it relieves them of the uncomfortable feeling of wondering who sits where. And it gives you the opportunity, or control, to balance out your table in a manner that will encourage conversation.

Take a piece of paper and draw a rectangle for the table. Then draw a box for where you want each chair to be. First, fill in where the hosts are going to be. Usually they are at the foot and head of the table. The person who is in charge of the kitchen would sit at the end that is closest to the kitchen. If there is a guest of honor, he or she would sit to the right of the host. Depending on your situation, a female guest of honor would sit to the right of a male host, and a male guest of honor would sit to the right of the female host. (This isn't written in stone, so do what works for you.) Now pencil in the rest of your guests, moving them around as many times as you need until you feel comfortable with the arrangement.

If your numbers work evenly, try to alternate men and women, and consider having couples sit separately. Give everyone a chance to talk with new people. Once you know where you want everyone to sit, put out a place card for each guest. If you don't want to use place cards, make sure you have your plan conveniently nearby so you'll be ready when the time comes for everyone to sit down.

Lighting and music help to set the tone and ambience for the party and should definitely be planned ahead of time. For nighttime parties, the ceiling or lamp lights and candlelight help to create the environment you want for a party. Dripless regular candles or votives are always a lovely addition. The music choices should complement your party. Have your playlist in order and ready before your guests arrive. When the party starts, have the volume turned low; as the party progresses, turn it up. In the beginning your guests are just getting comfortable and relaxed so you want the music to be low.

> Step 7 : Keeping a Time Table

If you're planning a party as if you're planning a to-do list, figuring out what needs to be done will fall in to place. Make yourself out a schedule.

UP TO A WEEK AHEAD OF TIME: Write out two separate lists: shopping and marketing list and a "to do" list. Try to organize the shopping list by categories so you don't wind up walking back and forth in the market. Try to arrange the "to-do" list in some sort of order so you don't forget any last-minute items. It is also extremely helpful to write out a basic cooking and serving schedule to help you keep everything moving forward.

Based on your personal schedule and when your open time is, you can do almost everything from buying the wine to cleaning the house days ahead of the party. If you happen to be at the store anyway, you might as well go ahead and buy the nonperishable items. Preparing and freezing the dessert or any side dishes is also a good time-saving idea.

ONE DAY AHEAD: While you can fit in the day-ahead and the day-of chores into one day, it's nice to be able to have everything planned so you can go to the grocery the day before the party. If you have any dishes that can be made the day before, then do so. You can also arrange the flowers for the tables. This is also the time to set out the platters, dishes, and serving utensils and create a plan for where everything will go. You might even want to have little pieces of paper on your platters that indicate what will be served on them. In the late afternoon or early evening, set your table.

DAY OF: Clean the salad greens and refrigerate them in open plastic bags. Cut up vegetables for all side dishes (except potatoes, which should be cut just before cooking to prevent blackening) and chill in plastic bags.

HOURS BEFORE: Get the coffee ready, including the cups and saucer, sugar bowl and cream pitcher. Complete whatever cooking can be done before the final preparation. Tidy up the house (don't forget the bathrooms), and then take a good hour to relax and get yourself ready.

AT THE PARTY: Greeting your guests at the door is your first priority. After everyone has arrived and been offered a drink, you can turn your attention to any last-minute cooking and reheating. It is important to keep track of all the little details and special touches that will keep everything running smoothly. Remember, a little planning goes a long way toward avoiding problems. A simple written schedule can bring you just the confidence you need that your party will be successful.

Don't be shy about asking a friend or two to lend a hand. It is a good idea for parties of eight or more (including the hosts) and will mean less time in the kitchen and more time with your guests for you. For larger parties, consider hiring someone to tend bar. The same individual can also assist with cleanup and other tasks that you may need help with.

And look out for the unexpected. Even at the most well-planned party, unanticipated problems are bound to happen. The secret is to stay composed and let the party flow as if nothing has happened while you deal with the situation discreetly. The most important thing to remember about throwing a party is that it's all about good friends, good food and lots of fun. It's an old saying worth repeating: Guests take their cue from the host.

> Step 8 : Pairing Wine with Food

Finally, it's time for some of the most important decisions: what wines you want and what would best complement your food. If you have questions about what tastes good with what, go to your local supermarket or specialty market and ask to speak with their wine expert. You can also go to one of the larger wholesale wine stores. Truly, it's all a matter of personal taste and choice. Begin by forgetting what you've heard about white with fish and red with meat. Instead, think about what you like. If you used wine as an ingredient in a dish you prepared, then you can serve that. (You should always cook with a wine you would drink.) As you read through the book, you will see that I have made several suggestions in this area. Please keep in mind that they are only just that, suggestions.

Simple. Classic. Parties.

> Step 8 : Pairing Wine with Food CONTINUED

A real wine enthusiast will taste a wine and think about the four basic qualities: body (does the wine feel light or heavy on the tongue?), intensity (is it bold and assertive, or delicate and mild?), general flavor (what kinds of tastes and aromas does it bring to mind: citrus, berry, apple, oak?), and flavor characteristics (is it dry or fruity; what is its level of acidity?).

But you don't have to think that way if you're not a wine enthusiast. Just think about all the different foods on your menu. Some people like to serve a different wine with each dish because they like variety. Keep in mind that food and wine are best together when their qualities are either similar (a full-bodied red served with a slow-cooked meat dish) or opposite (a sweet, light white matched with a spicy dish). When you're serving multiple wines, as a general rule, remember that they are better enjoyed when they go from light to heavy during the course of the meal, with whites served before reds, and dry wines before sweet ones.

> Dinner Party Tips

This may appear like a lot of work, but it really isn't. Like I said before, it shouldn't be stressful, and it doesn't have to be exhausting. The main thing is stay organized. Deal with one issue or decision at a time. Don't be afraid to ask a friend or two to assist you at the party. Friends want to help; they're just waiting to be asked.

Here are my tips for making your dinner party a success —

CUSTOMS: Every family has its own special customs that give us a sense of belonging. Many people celebrate Thanksgiving and Christmas every year. We often forget that there are so many more opportunities, like Valentine's Day, Easter, Passover, Mother's Day, and Father's Day, as well as Birthdays and Anniversaries. If you're not already celebrating any of these holidays, it's time to start. If you don't want to cook everything, make it a potluck. The host usually provides the entrée, and everyone else brings the rest. Let everyone bring what their specialty is.

PITCHING IN BEFORE THE MEAL: A lot of people would automatically ask a family member to lend a hand. There's really nothing wrong with asking a friend to help, too. Don't be shy; ask everyone to help. Have someone grab the salad, ask another person to grab the vegetables, and have another person grab the bread. People want to be helpful, and it makes your life easier, so why not?

EATERS WHO PRESENT A CHALLENGE: When you have a group of people over, you can expect a couple of dietary challenges, such as allergies or special diets. To try to avoid any problems when inviting a guest for the first time, I will ask them if they have any dietary restrictions. If they do, I write it down. I keep notes from all my parties. Not only do I keep track of any dietary issues, I also keep track of what people like and don't like. I also don't want to serve the same thing next time they come over, and I always like to have choices for my guests, such as two or three vegetables, and a couple of starches. At a major holiday like Christmas or Chanukah, I offer two entrées; that way there's something for everyone.

> Murphy's Law : It Will Happen!

Be prepared. You never know what's going to happen when you invite people over. The key is to rise about it all. Don't let your guests know that you are flustered. If you stay cool, calm and collected, your guests will be too.

Here are a few suggestions for handling the unexpected.

MECHANICAL DIFFICULTIES: Know that odds are whenever you invite a crowd over something is going to happen. Either the garbage disposal will break or the plumbing will backup. Try to smile, clean up the mess if there is one, then call your home warranty company (if you have one) and go on with the party.

BAD WEATHER: If you are planning an outdoor party, have a Plan B. If your home is big enough, just ask your friends to come in. If not, and you suspect that the weather is questionable the morning of, call a party rental company and rent a tent or canopy.

KITCHEN DISASTERS: Whether your roast gets overcooked or you drop it as you're taking it out of the oven, the show must go on. Save what you can, then check your refrigerator to see if you have any more ingredients for another side dish. If that doesn't work, call out for pizza. Remember, the important thing is being together, not what's on the menu.

GUEST ACCIDENTS: If something gets broken, quickly sweep it up and continue on with your party. Should wine get spilled, especially red, blot the stain with club soda, yell Mazel Tov, then place a napkin over it. You'd be surprised how all of a sudden everyone at the table has this little sigh of relief — not just because they weren't the ones who spilled anything, but because the traditional glass of spilled wine is done.

entertaining your way

chapter two

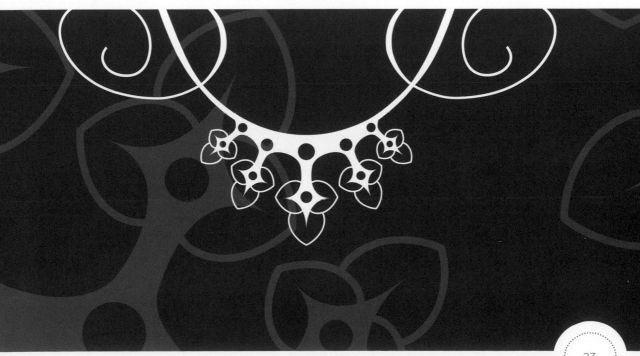

A cocktail party is the perfect vehicle to celebrate a special occasion, catch up with old friends or get better acquainted with new ones. One of the best things about a cocktail party is the ever-expanding guest list; you can invite as many people as you want because you don't have to worry about seating.

And that's just one of the benefits of throwing a cocktail party rather than a sit-down dinner. Beyond the flexibility of the guest list, there's less cooking involved, and if you want you can even set a time limit. It could be two hours or it could be four hours. They can be casual or formal, small intimate group or elbow-to-elbow and jumping. Think about what style feels right for the occasion and how much space you have, and then you can start planning.

But there really isn't any secret to planning a fun cocktail party. Just keep it simple with finger foods and easy drinks. Offer a few special cocktails, along with wine, beer, a relatively full bar and some nonalcoholic beverages. Serve a variety of hot and cold finger foods, either passed, set out at food stations, or both. Plus, your menu can include pre-made items as well. Keep portions small, certainly no more than two bites. And remember, you can never have too much ice or too many napkins.

cocktail parties

< Photo courtesy of Bria Tavakoli, New York City, NY

> Getting Organized

First, if there is an occasion you're celebrating — a birthday, an anniversary, a holiday — and you want to, choose a theme. Keep in mind that it doesn't have to be elaborate. If you really feel like taking it to the next level, come up with an idea that will bring everything together, including the invitations, any special décor, the cocktails, and your menu.

Next, choose where in your home you would like everyone to mingle and figure out a good time. Depending on where you live, the weather and time of year could be a factor. If you have a yard or patio, consider entertaining outdoors or hosting an indoor-outdoor party. Be creative with the space you have, but keep your eye on how traffic will flow from area to area.

Normally, cocktail parties are two to three hours. If you want your guests to stay a certain period of time, use the word "cocktails" and indicate the time, such as 6-8 p.m., on the invitation, so there's no confusion and they don't think that dinner will be served. This will help your guests plan their evening. If you don't care how long they stay, just indicate the requested arrival time and leave the invite open-ended.

If you are new to the world of cocktail-party hosting, you might want to make sure that you have prepared some or all of the food you want to serve at least once before the party, not only to make sure you like it, but also to be sure you can make it in a timely fashion. If you want to offer "signature" drinks or specialty drinks, practice making those, too.

The more cocktail parties you throw, the more comfortable you'll get and the easier it will become to entertain. With the ever-faithful mix of good friends, good food, good drinks and lots of fun, you'll soon discover, as so many people before you discovered, that cocktail parties are a fabulous way to get-together.

> Setting and Style

Creating style is not as complicated as you might think. The following four tips can transform your home into a warm, inviting party space. The main thing you want to do is maintain a consistent look.

SEATING: An old rule to entertaining is to not have as many chairs as guests (unless it's a sit-down dinner). The more chairs you have, the more likely that your guests will sit instead of walking around and talking. I have always been a fan of making different-size conversation areas. The key is to not make them too big; you want to keep them warm and inviting. They can be inside or outside on a patio; just make sure you figure about two to four square feet of space per standing person.

LIGHTING: If your party is inside, try dimming a few of your overhead lights. Lighten the food and bar spaces with the lamps you may already have in the room, and, of course, use candles, (dripless and unscented are usually best). If your party is outdoors, use candles of all shapes and sizes, and consider pillar or hurricane styles. If you have a backyard, hang ornamental lights above. I hang them from tree to tree or on the patio overhang for all of my parties. If you do use candles, ensure that they are a safe distance from all flammable products, especially fabrics.

FLOWERS: Pick up the flowers you need the day before your party. Most markets now have a wonderful selection of beautiful, colorful fresh flowers, and if the timing is right, perhaps there is a local farmers' market you can go to. There are no rules here, either: You can select multiple colors, or pick just one and add greenery. Put out as many arrangements as you like. However, by your bar area, and if you have a buffet, keep them small. You don't want them fighting for space. If you have space by your front door, you can even put some flowers or plants there. That gives your entrance a warm feeling. Also, if you are entertaining outside, put a few arrangements out there too.

MUSIC: What's a party without music? At the start of the party, the music should be soft and relaxing, and it should build as the evening goes on, to faster, livelier tunes. Make sure you do have a couple of small areas where the music isn't too loud, so your guests can go relax or have a quiet conversation, if they like.

> Finger Foods

Once you know what kind of party you're throwing — casual or formal, daytime or evening, themed or not — you can start planning your menu. Take a minute to think about what's in season, and consider whether your guests have any dietary issues. Your answers to these questions should help some recipe decisions fall into place.

Plan on five to six pieces per person, and try to include hot and cold items, a couple of items with a little kick, and of course, a couple of sweet items. Balance out your menu with store bought cheeses, dips, nuts and spreads.

Finger foods fit nicely on platters or trays and can be very simple to serve. But don't hold yourself to the traditional platters. Quite often I use marble for my cheese and fruit selections, or a wooden board covered with something decorative for my room temperature items.

There are going to be times when you pull out so many platters while you're thinking that you might not even remember which one was for what. As you take each one out, write on a small piece of paper what it is for, and then place it on the platter or bowl. Not only does it help you to keep organized, but also when someone asks if they can help put food out, it becomes very easy for them to see where the food should go. I do this for all my parties, even my small ones. When I first started doing this my friends would chuckle, thinking it's funny. Now many of them do it.

If you're only having a handful of people over, then you probably will only need one recipe per platter. If your party winds up being on the larger size, you might want to make two trays of each recipe, one to serve and one for backup, as needed. If you are serving any hot foods, you can use an electrically heated serving dish or one of those chafing dishes with a candle underneath. If you don't have either and you don't want to buy anything, then just use a platter you can stick in the oven to heat up. Make sure you put it on some sort of heatproof pad and place a little note next to it alerting your guests that the dish is hot.

The day before the party, walk around the areas you want to entertain in, and think about where you would like to place your food. The dining room table is an obvious choice. But what other areas do you have? Any flat surface will work. You can even use your kitchen table.

> Finger Foods (CONTINUED)

Putting your platters in separate locations will help the flow of your party — guests won't bunch up in one spot around the food. It's also best to have your bar area away from the food so that people who just want a drink don't have to wait in line with everyone going for food.

Regardless of where you have your platters, make sure you have lots of napkins and small plates in various spots. (Also, make sure you have cocktail forks or toothpicks if the food calls for it. Not everybody likes to use their fingers.) A well prepared host has at least double the plates and flatware as there are guests; it's very common for guests to put their plates down, or forget where they put them down, then find themselves looking for a fresh one. Paper products are fine: Many stores now carry beautiful sturdy ones that are appropriate for cocktail parties. Don't be afraid to use them, especially if you are having a large crowd.

> Setting Up The Bar

At a cocktail party, the drinks are considered your main event. If you want to be fun and different, offer one or two signature drinks along with the usual wine, beer, soft drinks, and water, in addition to the full bar, if you like. Place your bar in a space where it's easy for everyone to access. With larger groups, consider two separate locations: one for alcohol and one for non-alcoholic beverages.

Buy your party ice a couple of hours before your party. Figure about 1½ lbs. of ice per person, unless you need ice for chilling beer or champagne glasses, or for chilling cans of soda, in which case, you'll need more. When figuring what you need to buy in alcohol and mixers, it's best to stay away from the larger size bottles; once they are opened, their quality is compromised quickly. Smaller bottles like liters, fifths, or quarts will normally keep for an indefinite period of time.

If you want your bar to really be over the top, offer interesting garnishes, such as small pieces of fruit, assorted green olives, stuffed and not stuffed, herb sprigs, citrus twists, swizzle sticks, and decorative toothpicks. Put them in neatly arranged small bowls or containers on the bar area. Make sure you have a kitchen towel covering the bar area to absorb spills. Set up your glassware by type so it makes it easier for you or a bartender to grab what you need. If you have a bartender, you don't want him to waste time looking from side to side for the appropriate glass. Line up your bar tools, including a cocktail shaker, strainer, ice bucket, mixing spoons, and measuring devices. If you want, place champagne or white wine in a cooler or ice bucket to chill so it will be ready to serve.

Do something fun and different at your party and serve a few signature cocktails in addition to wine, beer and other drinks.

> Setting Up The Bar + Bar Essentials

Stock your bar with the following beverages:

WINE	SPIRITS	MIXERS
Champagne	Brandy/Liqueurs	Juices
Dessert wine	Gin	Sodas
Red wine	Rum	Water
White wine	Tequila	
	Vodka	
	Whisky	

BEER	ALCOHOL-FREE
6/12-packs	Beer/Wine
Keg	Coffee
	Soda
	Water

Then, add the following items:

- Cocktail shaker and strainer
- Bar spoon for stirring
- Ice bucket and tongs
- Pitchers for water and juices
- Small cutting board and paring knife (or prep your lemons and limes in the kitchen)
- Corkscrew and bottle opener
- Bar towels, lots of cocktail napkins
- Straws, cocktail toothpicks, swizzle sticks
- Electric blender (if you plan to offer blended drinks)

Simple. Classic. Parties.

> Garden Fresh Touches

SWIZZLE STICKS: At most parties, using fresh ingredients such as fruit sections and sprigs of herbs to form natural stirrers offers a unique burst of freshness. Select ingredients that will add a new dimension to the drink, yet still complement it.

A. Using a citrus stripper, very slowly cut long spirals of lemon or orange peel. Gently place a spiral over the side of the glass. Do this before you put in any ice or liquid. This would be perfect for a drink that had juice in it or a juice-flavored alcohol.

B. With a kitchen scissors, carefully snip rosemary branches into 3- to 4-inch lengths, depending on your glasses. Slide two fingers down the base of the sprig to take away the bottom leaves. This will be your handle. These would work well with gin or vodka cocktails.

C. Take a mango slice and peel all but one corner. Roll the peel back, and stick a cocktail toothpick in. This would complement any fruit or rum style cocktails.

FRUIT GARNISHES: There are no rules that dictate how fancy or plain a garnish has to be. Your goal is to add a little flair to your drink. The following garnishes can easily be made the day before and then stored in the refrigerator. Make sure they are in a covered container with a slightly moist paper towel on top.

D. Using a citrus stripper or vegetable peeler, slowly cut strips of lemon. Roll them tightly into a shape of a ball, then stick a cocktail toothpick through them. These look good with a juice-flavored cocktail like a Sunrise.

E. Take fresh fruit like nectarines or peaches and cut them into small cubes. Then take two pieces and stick a cocktail toothpick in them. A short time before you are ready to serve, roll them in sugar. Place the cubes so the rim is between the two cubes. You could have these for your fruity blended drinks like Daiquiris.

F. First peel a blood orange. Then very carefully segment it using a paring knife. Stick a cocktail toothpick into the whole wedge. Use with cocktails made with orange juice or orange liqueur, like a Blood Orange Martini.

GLASSWARE DECORATIONS: Easy touches can turn your regular glasses into festive party items. I've listed below just a few ideas for you to try.

G. Take a fancy toothpick or swizzle stick and tie a 4-inch piece of curled ribbon around the end. Then stick it in your glass for a special look.

H. For a glass that has a stem to it, wrap a 6-inch piece of curling ribbon around the stem. You can either curl it before you tie it, or curl it after.

I. Depending on the width of the glass, if it's tall, cut a piece of ribbon or raffia about 12- to 24-inches in length, and then wrap it around the bottom of the glass. It's probably best to knot it so it doesn't fall.

FRUIT DECORATED ICE CUBES: Making ice cubes that can be used for decoration is easy and beautiful. At Thanksgiving, I make fresh cranberry ice cubes. I fill the tray about halfway, drop in a couple of berries, then fill it up. You can use all kinds of fruits; these are just a few ideas.

J. With a paring knife, peel lemons, then cut them into sections. Drop a section into each cube. Leave a little bit of the section sticking up. Fill with water and freeze. These cubes would be great with a juice drink or a citrus alcohol.

K. Take a stripper and cut long pieces of one kind of citrus fruit, or a combination. Sprinkle a few slices in the tray, fill with water, and freeze. These would also be good with citrus flavored drinks.

L. Get any kind of fresh melon that you like. Take your melon scooper and scoop out pieces of melon. Drop the balls in the trays, fill with water, and freeze. These work well with tropical-themed cocktails.

> What Do I Need?

When planning a cocktail party, you want to make sure you have enough beverages on hand. The rule of thumb is one drink per person about every 45 minutes. For planning purposes, use these numbers as a guideline.

WINE AND CHAMPAGNE

BOTTLE SIZE	NUMBER OF OUNCES	NUMBER OF SERVINGS*
750 ml	25.4	5
1.5 liter	50.7	10
1 case	304.8	60

*1 serving = 5 ounces

SPIRITS

BOTTLE SIZE	NUMBER OF OUNCES	NUMBER OF SERVINGS*
750 ml	25.4	16
1 liter	33.8	22
1.75 liter	59.2	39

*1 serving = 1.5 ounces jigger

BEER

KEG SIZE	NUMBER OF OUNCES	NUMBER OF 16 OUNCES*
5 gallons	53	40
7.75 gallons	82	62
13.2 gallons	140	105
15.5 gallons	164	124

*1 serving = One 12-ounces bottle or 16-ounces pub glass

Simple. Classic. Parties.

> How do I calculate what I need?

Begin by thinking about how much your guests typically drink. Divide the number of guests between the types of beverages you plan to serve. For example, if you choose to offer wine, beer and alcohol-free beverages, then figure the number of servings for each category, calculating one drink every 45 minutes, or three drinks every two hours. Finally, match the total servings to the chart below for reference.

If you are not familiar with how much your guests may drink, it's best to figure high but still use the same number of guests for each category. For example, using the same 50 people above, with the same beverage offering, assume 25 will drink wine, 25 will drink beer and 25 will drink alcohol-free. It may seem that you're buying more than you need, but you don't want to run out.

EXAMPLE: 50 GUESTS FOR A TWO-HOUR EVENT

30 people will drink wine	3 drinks per person	equals 90 servings
10 people will drink beer	3 drinks per person	equals 30 servings
10 people will drink alcohol-free	3 drinks per person	equals 30 servings

IN THIS EXAMPLE, YOU WOULD NEED:

Wine	1.5 cases	for 90 servings
Beer	5 six-packs	for 30 servings
Alcohol-free wine	6-750 ml bottles	for 30 servings

> Do-Ahead Checklist

To give yourself more time to concentrate on the food and drinks the day of the party, take care of these tasks a day ahead:

- Vacuum and clean your party area.

- Check the bathroom. Make sure it has all the necessities: extra toilet paper, hand soap, hand towels, and tissues. It's also nice to have a lightly scented candle.

- If it's a chilly night, pick an area for hanging up coats, especially if you do not have a hall closet.

- Have candles and lights around your social area.

- Have all of your serving trays, platters and utensils out.

- Make sure you have plenty of small plates and napkins on the food tables for your guests.

- Place cocktail napkins not only in the bar area, but also around the room. You might also want to have coasters available.

- If you are using glass, rent or borrow extra if you are concerned that you might not have enough. For backup, always keep some disposable glasses on hand in case the glass ones break.

- Check out the outfit you want to wear and make sure it's ironed and ready to wear. You don't want to have to think about it at the last minute.

- Set a couple of ash trays outside just in case you have any guests that are smokers. Make sure they are placed well away from the door so the smoke won't come back in and your guests won't have to walk through it.

To give yourself more time to work on food and drinks the day of the party, take care of chores, like vacuuming, cleaning, and decorating the party spaces, one day ahead of time.

Simple. Classic. Parties.

entertaining your way

chapter three

You've done dinner parties and cocktail parties, and now you're ready to go to a whole new level of entertaining with something different. Why not host a wine and cheese party? This type of gathering is the ideal vehicle for people who really enjoy wine and cheese and would like to learn, or experience, more.

If just the thought of trying to put together the right wines and cheeses scares you, don't let it. As with everything in entertaining, there are no set rules, and it doesn't have to be perfect. In fact, when you throw a wine and cheese party, it really is a learning experience for everyone, including the host. One of the easiest parts about having this kind of party is that, if you want, you can look to other people, like the merchants at your local wine and cheese shops, to make your choices for you. Use the following steps as a guideline, and you'll be on the road to creating a fun and interesting experience at your next event.

wine & cheese party

> The Road to Enjoying Cheese

Developing one's own cheese range is really like continuing education. It's a road of frequent tasting and experimenting going past the basics and the common cheeses and expanding your cheese horizons where there are no limits. All it takes is a little desire and curiosity, and of course, a well-trained cheese merchant. He or she, can help guide you through all the questions and decisions.

The key isn't just tasting, but being open to new tastes. That's how you learn what you like and don't like. You can't judge the cheese by its appearance, or even its smell, for that matter.

It helps to visit the kinds of markets that will shave off a piece of cheese for you to sample, like a specialty market. High-noon on Saturday may not be the greatest time to ask for a taste, so go during less busy hours, when a staff member will be more available to offer information on the store's assortment. Farmer's markets are also an ideal place to learn about cheese. Many small cheesemakers bring their wares to these markets, and they encourage tastings and questions. In fact, one of the reasons they come to farmers' markets is to meet people and educate consumers about their cheeses so that word gets out, and you can learn a lot from them.

When you are asked what you like and don't like, be as specific as you can. Use words like creamier, sharper, more pungent or stronger. With the proper information, you can be pointed to the direction that's right for you.

> Assembling Your Cheese Tray

Before you decide on your cheeses, decide what you want to accomplish. Do you want to select a variety that you know everyone will enjoy? Or do you want to try and impress your friends with an elaborate assortment? Once you've established what you want, then aim for a variation in milks and textures.

Begin with what's referred to as a "gateway" cheese: a great starting cheese that most people enjoy and don't find intimidating. You gauge these cheeses by where you and your guests are in the world of cheese. If, for example, the most exciting cheese you have ever tried is Swiss cheese, then start with something simple like a Teleme, a semi-soft cheese made in Northern California. It was developed before World War II and is considered an American original.

Then you might be ready to jump to something like Epoisses, from the village of Epoisses in France, and a rustic sheep's milk cheese, which are often mild with a creamy texture, both characteristics that are appealing to a lot of people. Spanish Manchego, a famous cheese of Spain, is one possibility. Ossau-Iraty is another you should consider; made in the French Pyrenees Mountains, it has a buttery rich texture and richly nuanced flavor that pairs well with many white wines or a nice Merlot. You may notice that the wheels are different sizes. That is because the size varies from region to region.

You also might want to consider what is called a "stinky" washed-rind cheese. Don't shy away; their bark usually is worse than their bite. Something that has a powerful "stink" but is usually fairly mild in taste is a different idea — a nice Taleggio, which comes from the Lombardy region of Italy, almost always becomes a favorite once it's discovered that the flavor doesn't match with what its nose suggests.

It's very important that next to the cheese platter, you have a bread basket filled with sliced baguettes, small slices of whole grain, and whatever other fresh crusty breads look good to you. It's always nice to have some fruit and nuts that complement the flavors of the cheeses. For more suggestions, see "Cheese and Fruit Pairings" on page 52.

The main goal of a wine and cheese party is to try to get your guests to widen their cheese horizons. They will like some cheeses, and they won't like others. It doesn't matter as long as they have fun trying.

> Cheese Etiquette

Cheese has its full flavor when it's served at room temperature, and the texture becomes more giving so you can slice it. A small refrigerated wedge will take about an hour to come to room temperature, and larger pieces will require more time. The weather and the temperature in your home may have some influence on this, too.

When you take the cheese out of the refrigerator, you must unwrap it right away. Don't just set it down and come back to it. Cheese can release moisture as it warms, and you don't want the wrapping to hold it in. At this point, it is essential that you protect the cheese from drying out. Cover it with a cheese dome or glass bowl, or whatever you have. Blue cheeses may release a little more moisture as they come to room temperature. If they do, gently pat them down with a paper towel before serving.

Well-made cheese can stand on its own and needs little enhancement. That being said, a simply decorated platter or cheese board can make your cheese more inviting. Choose a surface that is easy for your guests to cut on, such as wood, marble, granite, or a wicker tray with a glass insert. Don't try to get as many cheeses as you can on one board. Leave room for your guests to maneuver. If you have lots of cheeses, you can always have a second board. If you have access to fresh large or decorative leaves, they make an attractive lining for under the cheese.

Remove any paper or foil wrappers, but leave the rinds in place. The rind is the cheese's natural wrap and is part of the integrity of the cheese. Guests can cut it away themselves if it is inedible or they choose not to eat it.

It's important to have a separate knife for each cheese to avoid cross contamination. Some aged cheeses with concentrated flavors and a harder texture are delicious when shaved, so if you may want to have a cheese plane on hand, too. With Parmigiano-Reggiano have a blunt knife that can break away the cheese into chunks, as slicing it compromises its texture. Many specialty and cookware stores sell a trowel-bladed tool made especially for these hard cheeses.

When you cut the cheese, it's important to try to keep the wedge as close as possible to its original shape. You also want to keep it looking appetizing for the next person. The goal is for each person to be able to have a bite of the whole cheese from the core to the rind, assuming they want some of the rind. Make your slice going the length of the cheese, not just cutting across one of the corners.

> Best Time for Cheese

A cheese is at its best when it is first cut. Once a cheese is open to the air, and especially when it's been sliced, its unavoidable deterioration begins. The quality also suffers each time the cheese goes in and out of the refrigerator. So make sure you wrap it properly before you put it in the refrigerator, so you don't have to remove it until your party preparation begins.

High-moisture cheeses, such as Feta or fresh goat cheese, do well in an airtight plastic container. All but the driest cheeses should be wrapped in waxed paper and placed in a lidded container. You can keep more than one kind of cheese in the same container, although blue cheeses should be kept isolated to prevent their molds from traveling. You may also want to keep washed-rind cheeses separate to avoid infusing other cheeses with their strong aroma. Dry cheeses, such as Parmigiano-Reggiano, no longer have much moisture to lose, so a tight foil wrap is fine.

> Personalizing Glasses & Carafes

When having a wine and cheese party, to bring your planning up a notch, help your guests keep track of their wine glasses. Here are a few homestyle ideas:

A Use nontoxic foliage to label the different types of wine glasses, such as citrus flowers for white wine glasses and small olive branches for red wine glasses.

B Cut out a small shape from a piece of light-colored card stock. Write a guest's name on each tag and make a hole in the tag with a hole punch.

C Use a length of twine to tie a piece of foliage and a tag to the stem of each guest's glass. This is a great way to achieve a special look while being practical at the same time.

D Write out the recommended cheeses to pair with each wine on a tag, and use the twine to tie it along with a piece of foliage to the matching carafe or wine bottle.

When you're choosing a wine to go with cheese, your main goal should be to "do no harm" to the taste of the wine.

> Pairing Wine and Cheese

Regardless of why you are choosing wine, whether it be for a cheese platter for all to enjoy or just for a glass for yourself with a slice of cheese, your main goal remains the same: to "do no harm" to the taste of the wine. This is a saying a sommelier told me a long time ago. When we are sharing our ideas about what makes an effective wine and cheese match, we mean that the cheeses do not have a negative impact on our wine enjoyment — meaning, the wine is just as delicious on its own as with the added flavor of the cheese.

In fact, the cheese is the leading mate in this combination, and your observation of it is most likely not going to change based on the wine you are enjoying at the moment.

Here are a few fundamentals for you to consider when making your choices:

REGION. Offering cheese and wine from the same region gratifies us from an emotional standpoint. Still, there are a number of cheeses that come from areas where wine isn't even made, and just because something is regional, it isn't always the best.

MOLD. The veins of mold in blue cheeses strip most dry white and red wines of their fruit. A sweet wine is usually the better choice. The more powerful and salty the blue flavor, the richer the dessert wine should be. Surprisingly, chilled sparkling wines can hold their own with many blue cheeses.

INTENSITY. For subtle wines, choose more subtle cheeses. Full-bodied wines can handle the stronger-flavored cheeses. That's why young cheeses like fresh goat cheese usually go with the younger-flavored wine that's lean and fruity, like Sauvignon Blanc or Chenin Blanc. The reverse is the aged cheeses, such as Parmigiano-Reggiano, which with their sharp concentration are best with a full bodied wine.

TEXTURE. Is the cheese creamy and does it gently coat your tongue, or is it just firm and dry and perhaps crumbly when you chew it? Is the wine crisp and refreshing, like Sauvignon Blanc? Or is it a full-bodied red like Cabernet Sauvignon? Matching textures can be a wise plan. However, if you feel like being daring, sometimes contrasting textures can work, too.

ACIDITY. Like so many foods and drinks, cheeses and wines have acidity. When you choose a cheese with a strong acidity factor such as cheddar, it is a smart idea to balance it with a wine of similar acidity, like a Bordeaux or Zinfandel.

SWEETNESS. When we say a cheese is sweet, we don't mean that literally. Excluding the freshest of cheeses like cottage cheese, cheese has no calculable amount of sugar. Regardless, we sense that some cheeses do have a sweet finish. As an example, there's a full bodied, yet mellow, British territorial cheese, Lincolnshire Poacher, that can leave that impression. A dessert wine with nut and caramel notes like Madeira can be especially delicious with such cheeses. Surprisingly, this cheese also pairs well with British ales.

There are a couple of wines that test the experience of a true cheese enthusiast. Beware of heavily oaked wines, particularly oaky whites, as they rarely pair well with cheese. Be cautious of wines with a high tannin level; they have a tendency to dry out your mouth a little at first taste. They pair best with dry, aged cheeses such as Parmigiano-Reggiano.

> Pairing Suggestions

WINE	CHEESE
Full-bodied reds (like Bordeaux)	Tangy, soft ripened cheeses (Brie, Camembert)
Spicy, full-bodied reds (Cabernet Sauvignon, Zinfandel)	Sharp, salty cheeses (Vermont White Cheddar, Parmigiano-Reggiano)
Fruity, medium-bodied reds (Pinot Noir, Barbera)	Semisoft, mild goat cheeses
Full-bodied whites (Chardonnay, Viognier)	Mild, creamy cheeses (Beaufort, Gruyere)
Light, fruity whites (Sauvignon Blanc, Pinot Gris)	Tangy herbed or plain fresh goat cheese
Crisp, spicy wines (Gewurztraminer, Riesling)	Salty aged cheeses (Manchego, Pecorino)
Sweet fortified wines (Port, Sherry, Madiera)	Pungent blue cheeses (Gorgonzola, Stilton, Spanish Cabrales)
Sweet white wines (Sauternes, late-harvest Riesling)	Soft, creamy cheeses (Muenster, Taleggio)

> Pairing Suggestions

BEER	CHEESE
Amber Ale	Cotswald Parmigiano-Reggiano Swiss
Belgian Ale	Stilton
Blonde Ale	Brie Camembert
Brown Ale	Manchego Swiss
Hoppy Pilsner	Gouda Havarti Jack
India Pale Ale	Dry Jack Parmigiano-Reggiano Provolone
Lambic	Chevre
Pale Ale	Cheddar Havarti Mahon
Pilsner Style Lager	Brie Mild Cheddar Mozzarella
Porter	Blue Gouda Muenster
Stout	Cheddar Blue Dubliner
Wheat Beer	Mozzarella Swiss

Simple. Classic. Parties.

< Photo courtesy of FireFly Farms, Inc.

> Cheese and Fruit Pairings

CHEESE	FRUIT	NUTS/CONDIMENT
Asiago	figs, grapes, melon, strawberries, dried apricot	pistachios
Blue	apples, pears, pineapple, dried cherries, dried cranberries, dried figs, dates	walnuts
Brie	melon, strawberries	almonds
Cheddar (mild)	apples, grapes, raisins	hazelnuts
Cheddar (aged)	apples, pineapple	almonds
Cheese curds (fresh)	apples, grapes	prepared mustard
Colby	melon, strawberries	hot/sweet mustard
Emmentaler	apples, pears	chutney
Feta	figs, grapes	sun-dried tomatoes, olives, honey
Gouda	apricots, cherries	prepared mustard, pickled onions
Gruyere	apples, figs, grapes, melons, pears, dates	walnuts, membrillo
Havarti	apples, grapes, plums, raisins	almonds, roasted red peppers
Mascarpone	raspberries	chocolate curls
Monterey Jack	apples, citrus fruits, grapes, kiwi	sweet or hot pepper jelly
Mozzarella	melon, peaches, oranges	prepared mustard
Muenster	apples, grapes	prepared mustard
Parmesan	grapes, plums, dried figs	walnut
Provolone	figs, grapes, pears	prepared mustard, roasted red peppers
Ricotta	figs, pears	honey, pine nuts
Swiss	apples, grapes, pears, strawberries	prepared mustard, cashews

> Seasonal Fruits

SEASON	FRUITS
Spring	cherries, grapefruits, limes, mandarins, pomelos, raspberries, rhubarb, strawberries
Summer	apricots, blackberries, blueberries, boysenberries, cherries, figs, melons, nectarines, peaches, plums, raspberries, rhubarb, strawberries
Fall	apples, figs, grapes, kiwifruits, melons, pears, pomegranates, rhubarb
Winter	dates, grapefruits, grapes, kiwifruits, limes, pears, pomegranates, pomelos, quinces, tangerines
Year-round	bananas, lemons, oranges

Simple. Classic. Parties.

> Cheese 101

CHEESE TYPE	DESCRIPTION
Soft Ripened	These are cheeses maturing from the outside in, meaning the cheese at the outside edge is further ripened than the center. They usually are soft, creamy and buttery, occasionally runny; mostly they are round in shape and somewhat flat. The white, fluffy ones have what is referred to as a "bloomy" rind that develops from small mold spores (good ones called penicillin candidum) and is totally edible. Some people feel they have a lightly earthy, mushroomy quality.
	Examples: Brie and Camembert are the most common. There's also Saint Nectaire, Chaource, Explorateur, Coulimiers and Reblochon from France, and French triple cream, such as Saint Andre.
Semi-Soft	These are cheeses commonly described as "beginner's taste" level, and they are familiar and loved by all. They tend to go well with almost anything and are considered very good melting cheeses. They're relatively high in moisture yet still hold their shape and are not runny. They range from very mild to pretty intense. Heartier ones are often made from raw milk.
	Examples: Colby, Fontina, Havarti, Monterey Jack, Port Salut, Edam, Montasio, Chihuahua, Teleme or Brick.
Firm/Hard	With more time aging and less moisture, these embody a wide range of styles and flavors. They often are defined with words like sharp, buttery, fruity and winey — as in going well with wine.
	Examples: Swiss and cheddar, such as Appenzell and Emmenthal from Switzerland, English Cheshire and Leicester, French Cantal and aged Dutch Gouda, Dry Jack, Gruyere and anything related to Parmesan.
Natural Rind	These develop their outsides, a rind, naturally by dry aging. No molds or microflora, which are invisible to the naked eye, are added, and the rind is not washed as it ages. Since they are often aged for several weeks, they often are made from raw milk and can create a whole lot of flavor.
	Examples: Tome de Savoie, Mimolette, English Stilton, or Lancashire.
Washed Rind	Smelly cheeses have a bark worse than their bite. Their strong aromas can scare the inexperienced, but these cheeses generally have subtle distinctions or variations, and are complex and less frightening than they smell. As they age, the cheeses are washed with anything from beer to wine, molds, brine or any mixture of ingredients; the resulting rind is frequently orange in color. They can be tangy, nutty and not quite runny inside but often are milder and sweeter than the strong aromas suggest.
	Examples: Epoisses, Taleggio, Livarot, Pont l'Eveque.

> Cheese 101

CHEESE TYPE	DESCRIPTION
Blue	These are ripened from the inside out. Blue/green veining is created when Penicillium Roqueforti mold is added to the milk or curd. These are friendly molds that create distinctive flavors that range from milk, sweet and mushroomy to overpowering. Even though there are various styles, both raw-milk and pasteurized, this family of cheeses leans toward salty and bold as opposed to demure, with textures that can vary from creamy to firm to crumbly. Cow's milk, goat's milk and sheep's milk are all used, with goat's milk the least often used.
	Examples: Cashel, Blue, French Roquefort and Bleu de Bresse, Italian Gorgonzola, English Stilton, Saga, Cabrales, Cambozola and American Maytag.
Goat and Sheep-Milk	The tanginess of these cheeses includes another element of taste. Your choices range anywhere from crumbly aged chevre from France to fresh American goat cheese with herbs to firm sharp sheep-milk cheese from Spain.
Pasta Filata	The definition is pulled curd — or paste — in Italian, and there is no better way to explain the process used to make these wonderful cheeses. Curds, after soaking in the whey that has separated out of the milk, are stretched and pulled like taffy before they are shaped, often into balls and sometimes into braids. A favorite cheese for adding tomatoes and fresh basil, the flavor of pasta filata cheeses tends toward milky and sweet, with an underpinning of acidity for balance. Young and milky, mild to aged and tangy — these cheeses have textures all their own.
	Examples: Mozzarella, burrata, Scamorza, Caciocavalo, strong cheese, Oaxaca, Kasseri.
Fresh	Not aged, but slightly cured, these cheeses are frequently high in moisture, creamy, milky, soft and like other fresh dairy foods, needing to be refrigerated and eaten in a timely manner. Although a simpler cheese, a definite favorite of many.
	Examples: Cream cheese, mascarpone, ricotta, chevre, feta, fromage blanc, burrata, quark or cottage cheese.

When you're learning about cheese, be open to new things. You can't judge a cheese by its appearance or smell, only by its taste.

Simple. Classic. Parties.

> Cheese Glossary

Alpine	From the tastes of those high-mountain cheeses, usually nutty, sharp, natural wheels that age well and melt beautifully.
Aromatic	It's all in the nose.
Artisan	Made carefully by someone, somewhere. This has become a very popular term. Unfortunately, it gets overused and misused.
Assertive	Strong, forceful
Buttery	Feeling, flavor, and creamy; a popular style of certain Vermont cheeses.
Caramel	A cooked flavor, like a delicious very aged Gouda.
Chalky	Not in a bad way, it's more of a feeling you get in your mouth as opposed to the taste. This often would apply to goat cheeses.
Cheddaring	It's the process when they cut and press the curd while making cheddar.
Chevre	A frequent name used for goat cheese; it's from the French word for goat.
Creamy	Feels and tastes like dried, heavy cream in your mouth. It's the goal of many soft-ripening cheeses.
Earthy	With a solid base aroma, but should never taste dirty.
Farmstead	Cheeses that are made in the same location where the animals that supply the milk live.
Floral	Like wild flowers and sweet grasses.
Fruity	Anything from the light taste of fresh fruit, like apples, pears, peaches, and grapes, to name a few.
Goaty	One of those things you have to experience to identify.
Grainy	A texture, a form of crystallization, as in aged Parmesan.
Grassy	A taste that can be a positive flavor in a well-balanced aged cheese.
Herbal	See above, but with more explicit recognizable fresh herb flavors like dill, rosemary, tarragon, or thyme.
Mild	Predictable and not bad except when it is too bland. But in some cheeses, it is delicious.
Milky	In an enjoyable fresh way.

> Cheese Glossary

Mushroomy	With a slight suggestion of a fresh raw mushroom taste.
Musky	Refer to "goaty"
Nutty	As in almonds, hazelnuts or walnuts.
Organic	As in certified; the feed, the milk, the animals, the cheese.
Pungent	Strong aroma.
Rennet	The common term for the cheese starter that is traditionally made from enzymes from the stomach lining of a suckling animal. Vegetable rennet also is used in many cheeses.
Ripe	An overall cultural belief as to the perfect spot of aging; when a cheese is at its best.
Rubbery	Acceptable if it's at a minimum with a good taste, but a cheese shouldn't be too bouncy.
Runny	That wonderful creamy texture that makes Brie such a favorite.
Rustic	Highly individual taste but an appropriate description.
Salty	Good, bad or just right.
Sharp	As in a well-aged cheddar or tangy Swiss.
Smoky	Best in naturally cold-smoked cheeses like cheddar or Gouda.
Spicy	The way Zinfandel is for wine and some washed rind cheeses can appealingly be. Something with a little kick; perhaps the cheese has peppers or hot spices in it.
Starter	Like rennet, only from plants, some thistles, or the twigs that hold a fig to a tree. Something that gets the solid to separate from the whey and moves things along toward becoming cheese. This may be developed in a laboratory, but using thistles sounds more romantic.
Stinky	A washed rind cheese that is usually stronger on the outside than the taste is on the inside.
Tangy	With a slightly sour, acidic snap.
Tart	Cleanly acidic.
Weepy	With liquid coming out. When applicable, this can refer to the eyes (those gas-made holes in Swiss type cheeses), as they "tear." A perfect moment in some cheeses' lives.
Zippy	Some positive blends of slightly tart, tangy and occasionally sweet.

Simple. Classic. Parties.

> Do-Ahead Checklist

To give yourself more time to concentrate on the wine and cheese party, take care of these tasks a day ahead:

- Visit a good cheese store or cheese section at your favorite market a few days before the party to taste a variety of hard and soft cheeses, so you can make well-informed choices. Tell them your likes and dislikes, too.

- Ask a trusted wine merchant for red, white, and dessert wine recommendations to pair with your cheeses. If you can time it right, some specialty stores have wine tastings. That's an excellent way to learn about new wines.

- Decorate serving trays and platters with grape leaves and clusters, fig leaves, or olive branches. Check to see what kind of trees or flowers you have in your backyard.

- Set out the cheeses on a marble slab or cutting board covered with a kitchen towel a few hours before the party so they come to room temperature. Don't forget to put out a knife for each cheese.

- If you're having a wine theme, put cut flowers in wine carafes of varying sizes around your social area and on your food tables.

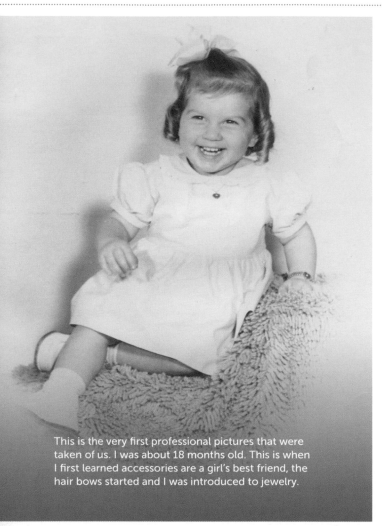

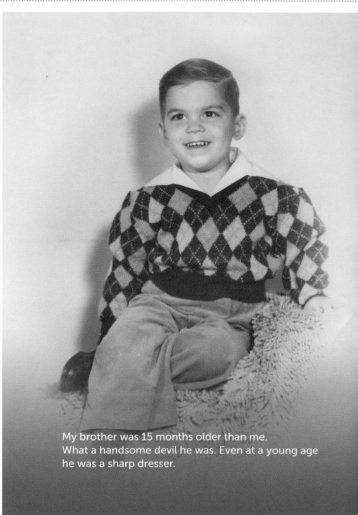

This is the very first professional pictures that were taken of us. I was about 18 months old. This is when I first learned accessories are a girl's best friend, the hair bows started and I was introduced to jewelry.

My brother was 15 months older than me. What a handsome devil he was. Even at a young age he was a sharp dresser.

Roy Rogers and Dale Evans don't have anything on us.

The Leibovitz Family: Florence, Steven, Harold and Andrea.
Your typical 50's family, daddy's little girl and mommy's little man. When we were little,
my mom always had us beautifully dressed. We were quite the show stoppers everywhere we went.

I was told that this was the first serious photo my parents personally took of us when I first joined the family. I don't know what my brother was thinking, but for me, it was love at first sight.

I am 8 years old here, a fashion statement even as a child.
My brother doesn't look too bad either.

entertaining your way

chapter four

Sometimes when I'm relaxing on my back patio, enjoying a refreshing peach bellini or sipping a fresh mimosa, I ask myself why I didn't call a few friends and ask them to join me for brunch. It's such a special way to spend some leisurely time with friends. It doesn't hurt that brunch is also an extremely versatile meal to prepare for guests: It can top off a morning of sports or can celebrate a special holiday.

In fact, a plentiful brunch for friends offers a unique variation from the normal evening gatherings. As the sun rises higher in the blue sky, your guests come join you in your inviting kitchen for a fresh cup of coffee, while you finish getting your food ready. Displayed on your countertops, steps away from where everyone is standing, you have your delicious buffet highlighting everyone's favorites. For a little decoration, you might have placed a few herb topiaries around, and a bowl of seasonal fresh fruit instead of flowers. Or, if you have your own garden, you may have vases filled with freshly cut flowers, rounding off that "at home" feeling. Sometimes the sunshine or blue skies can be a special guest, particularly in springtime or the early months of summer when the air is warm and still and everything around you makes you feel like you want to say "what a day!" It's the kind of weather that couldn't be any better if you ordered it, a perfect day for a get-together.

brunches

> Brunch Ideas

Brunch can be as simple or as extravagant as you like. For those impromptu occasions, with the right ingredients on hand, you can have control of your menu. If you feel like sleeping a little longer, you needn't worry, because you can choose from an assortment of great choices hidden away in your fridge or panty. Even finicky eaters can be fed and pampered without stressing the cook.

As we all know, there are some of us who like to indulge ourselves, or our guests, to foods that are sweeter than we would normally serve at lunch or dinner, such as muffins, fruit pastries, coffee cakes, cereal topped with sugar and/or cinnamon, or a stack of pancakes with lots of warm syrup. Then there are those who like something salty and smoky like bacon, lox, sausage, or cheese. Some brunch foods are soft and creamy, some are moist and juicy, and others are crunchy or chewy. If brunches are your favorite gathering and you either host them regularly or would like to, then you'll want to get your kitchen in order with breakfast foods and the necessary items I have detailed below.

EGGS: We all know to store eggs in the refrigerator to keep them fresh and delicious. There are some cooks who say it's all right to keep them out on a short-term basis because their shells keep them protected. I personally prefer refrigeration. If you have the opportunity to get farm-fresh eggs, by all means try them. The fresher the egg, the better the flavor. Sometimes, like in a specialty market, you can find cage-free eggs, eggs enriched with omega-3, eggs from hens fed a vegetarian diet, and certified organic eggs.

Eggs can definitely stand on their own. However, you will discover that eggs are a very important ingredient in countless other dishes, as well, like pastries and breads. Eggs can also give baked goods a beautiful rich color and a shiny glaze. Just brush any homemade baked goods lightly with an egg wash, made from whole eggs, a mixture of whole eggs and yolks, or just yolks combined with water, milk or cream, before they go into the oven.

DAIRY: From a splash of cream or half-and-half for a cup of coffee to tart buttermilk in your favorite pancake batter to cream cheese on a bagel, brunch dishes always demand a variety of dairy products. Many of them will keep in the refrigerator for several days. Milk, cream, yogurt, and soft cheeses usually have a date somewhere on the label. This date stamp for the most part is for the market as it indicates the last date that the product is fresh enough for sale. This is also your guideline as to how long it has been sitting.

BREADS AND PASTRIES: The word "bread" kind of says it all. Freshly baked breads, muffins, bagels, and pastries are a necessity at any brunch. If you have a good source for baked goods, like a market or bakery, then you should definitely offer them to your guests. Depending on where you live, good quality bagels can be hard to find, but if you are a fan, it's worth the search. When you find them, buy plenty so that you can have some on hand to serve and some to store for later in the freezer. When I buy extra bagels, I cut them in half, individually wrap them in plastic wrap and then put them in a freezer bag before I freeze them. That way, you can grab one at a time, or even half, if you like.

Most baked goods are best kept at room temperature in the bag they came in, unless they have a filling made with eggs or other highly perishable ingredients. If you are buying items from a bakery, tell them when you will be needing everything and ask them to wrap them appropriately. Frozen baked goods thaw relatively fast at room temperature. For bagels, muffins, or rolls, defrosting will take approximately 1 to 2 hours. (Alternately, you can take them out of the freezer the night before.) You can freshen up thawed baked goods in a warm oven, at about 300 to 325 degrees, depending on your oven, for a few minutes, but do not put them in the microwave, as they can become chewy.

SPREADS AND SYRUPS: Some traditional brunch stand-bys — toast, bagels, pancakes, and waffles — scream out for a topping. Having a nice selection on hand is a wonderful way to add variety to your meal and take it to the next level. Jams, jellies, and marmalades can last unopened in a dark, dry cupboard for up to one year. They can also become an ingredient for a sweet omelet. Molasses and honey can last for several months in the cupboard, even if they have been opened, as long as they are tightly capped.

Flavored butters can be sweet or savory. You can take the time to shape each pad, or you can serve them in little pots or crocks. Flavored butters also freeze well. A good technique for freezing is to roll the butter into the shape of a log, wrap well using something like wax paper, and then place a label that you have written the date on somewhere on the top. Then simply slice off pieces as needed.

Maple syrup stores well when kept in the refrigerator, where it could last for several months. Make sure you wipe any drips away from the sides, bottom, lid and opening of the jar when you are done with it.

Sauces, like purees, are very easy to make. They can be stored in your refrigerator for up to two weeks or in the freezer for up to four months. Curds are a little trickier and are probably the most perishable spreads because they include egg yolks. Unfortunately, they do not freeze well, but they can be refrigerated for up to one week. Fruit curds that you buy in a market can be stored for several months if they are unopened. Once you open the jar, refrigerate it, and use within two weeks.

Nut butters such as peanut, almond, or cashew, are a unique substitute to your normal butter as a spread for toasts or rolls. Freshly ground nut butters will probably separate as they sit; make sure you give them a quick stir to bring them back together just before serving. Keep freshly ground nut butters in the refrigerator. If you don't feel like making fresh nut butters, you can buy them from some markets. Because they are commercial brands, they are homogenized and made so they won't separate; they can be safely kept in a cupboard in all but the warmest of weather.

FRUIT: Always keep fresh fruit on hand. It's just not good for company, but it's delicious and healthy too. You can add sliced bananas into a bowl of smooth and creamy yogurt, cut thin wedges of melon or scoop them into bite-size balls, or prepare fresh or dried fruits to add into sauces and compotes. Fruit salads are always a delicious and welcome treat that can be made ahead. Besides that, a piled high bowl of fresh fruit makes a beautiful and useful centerpiece.

When berries, peaches, and cherries are in season in your local market, make sure you buy plenty to freeze. Blueberries and cranberries freeze wonderfully; simply put them in freezer bags, seal, and store. The more delicate berries such as raspberries, strawberries and blackberries, should be laid out in a single layer on a cookie sheet and placed on a shelf in the freezer, uncovered, until solid. Then it is safe to transfer the berries to freezer containers or freezer bags. If you're putting them in a bag, do your best to get all the air out. As a rule, there is no need to thaw frozen berries before adding them to pancakes or muffins. Just make sure there isn't a lot of ice around them.

Dried fruits are also something to consider. Most local markets will have a wide variety for you to choose from. Make sure you stock up on favorites like raisins, currants, prunes, cranberries and cherries. They give a sweet-tart punch to baked goods.

Simple. Classic. Parties.

> Brunch Ideas (CONTINUED)

VEGETABLES: Potatoes, onions, garlic, shallots, and tomatoes are all important basic vegetables for any brunch menu. Store them in a dry, cool, dark cupboard. Lettuces, leafy greens, seasonal delicacies such as asparagus and other farm fresh finds absolutely should be used as quickly as possible. Some will last a day or two if they are kept in the refrigerator. Tomatoes can be kept on hand as fresh, sun-dried, and canned. Some cooks say you should never refrigerate a tomato as it ruins the flavor, but I always refrigerate my tomatoes. It's a question of taste. Salsa has become a popular brunch accessory to give a plain egg dish, or a potato a little pizzazz.

MEATS, POULTRY AND FISH: Adding some meat, poultry or fish to your menu gives the meal more stamina. Keep portions a little smaller than you would have for lunch or dinner. Rich, smoky sausages, bacon, ham, salmon, and trout are traditional classic breakfast favorites. At a brunch, you can be more creative and include a whole roasts or a turkey, which you can carve at the table, like something you might see at an expensive champagne brunch at a restaurant or hotel.

BEVERAGES: Whether you're partial to a hot pot of coffee made with freshly ground beans, a delicate pot of hot tea, or a cup of rich, creamy hot chocolate, hot beverages are a must. Make sure you also have cold beverages, such as juices, juice blends, smoothies, and, if you like, cocktails. Fresh-squeezed juices (single fruits or blends) can be made with a juicer or blender. However, bottled juices and frozen concentrates are easy to keep on hand, and less work. Other non-alcoholic beverages to have on hand are water, still and sparkling, and seltzer.

Then there's champagne, wine, and spirits such as gin and vodka, which are in many brunch cocktails. You might also have brandy and rum on hand if you are doing any of the baking or making compote yourself; it's good for plumping any dried fruits you might be using.

> Do-Ahead Checklist

To give yourself more time to concentrate on the food and drinks the day of the party, take care of these tasks a day ahead:

- Decide what your menu will be.

- Pick a spot in your kitchen that will be easy to serve from, leaving yourself enough counter space for a work area if needed.

- Put the flatware and napkins in a lined basket. If you have the time, wrap each place setting with a napkin, then tea ribbon around it.

- Get out the bowls and/or plates you would like your guests to use.

- Set out your stemware or glasses for juices or drinks. As an extra touch, have a pitcher for each juice.

- Position the mugs or cups close to the coffee pot, along with a pitcher for cream or milk, a bowl for sugar and a few spoons.

- Make sure your toaster is in a convenient spot that your guests can reach. Place a cutting board next to it, along with a bread knife. Also have table knives for the butter, cream cheese, jam, or peanut butter nearby. Make sure you have enough knives out so each spread has its own.

- If you plan to make pancakes, waffles, muffins, or biscuits, measure out the dry ingredients into a bowl and cover with plastic wrap. Mix up the wet ingredients and keep them in the refrigerator. Your muffins and biscuits should be ready just before your guests arrive. Your pancakes and waffles can also be made ahead and then warmed up briefly in the microwave. To bring this to the next level, having an area where you can make them fresh, as needed, in front of the guests can be fun, too.

Simple. Classic. Parties.

entertaining your way

chapter five

These days, tea is customarily enjoyed from mid-to late afternoon. In England, many people enjoy afternoon tea. It also comes in handy as a way to entertain business associates. It's a little nosh to enjoy after lunch and before dinner. But it doesn't have to be fancy or extravagant. The traditional finger sandwiches or small cakes, along with a delicious cup of tea, will do just fine. A classic tea party has timeless attraction. If you feel like having some friends over and you want to keep it on the simple side, a tea party can be the way to go. It's also a perfect vehicle for a bridal or baby shower or a birthday.

Your menu is set and ready before your guests arrive. You can either set it out on a buffet table or have the food directly placed on the tables. The only thing you have to concern yourself with during the party is the tea. If you serve buffet style, there is virtually no limit to the amount of people you can invite; just figure out how many will fit in your social areas. Maybe there are just one or two special people that you would like to spend some quality time with. You can have a more elegant affair, like the kind you find at the fancier hotels, or it can be very casual with just a pot of tea and some homemade cookies. Keep in mind planning small conversation areas will offer your guests a warm inviting spots to talk. When deciding which plates your guests will use for food, a smaller size is best so they can balance the plate on their laps if need be.

tea parties

> Afternoon Tea Traditions

There is no more classic English custom than the traditional serving of afternoon or high tea.

There's an old story that Anna, the 7th Duchess of Bedford received credit for the original custom of the afternoon tea dating back to the early 19th century. The story goes that the duchess usually had dinner late in the evening and consequently became hungry in the afternoon. To fight off her hunger pains she would have bread, butter, sweets and tea brought to her room. People started thinking it was a great idea, the word spread, and the afternoon tea was born.

What was called the "at home" tea soon spread all over many areas of England. Back then they actually sent out notices to people indicating the time that tea would be served. On occasion there would be some form of entertainment, but the main purpose was for everyone to get together and talk, and of course, catch up on the local gossip. The hostess would stay home all day just to greet guests and serve tea and the traditional foods. If you received an "at home" invitation, it was assumed that you would attend. The hostess only wanted RSVPs for regrets. On any given day there was at least one person having an "at home" day. This was how community connections were developed and women had the opportunity to see each other practically every day at different houses.

The old tradition of the "at home" is long gone, but the serving of afternoon or high tea lives on. Many prominent hotels have a High Tea from about 3 to 5 p.m. Some cities even have charming little tea shops. I've heard of a place in Yorkshire called Betty's. They have a worldwide reputation for having "the" high tea foods.

> Serving Afternoon Tea

Afternoon tea customarily begins with tasty finger sandwiches like smoked salmon, cucumber or egg and mustard cress. The next course usually consists of delicious scones that would be served with jam and cream or clotted cream. The meal concludes with a variety of small cakes.

In Britain, they may also offer breads like English muffins, hot buttered toast, or crumpets. In Scotland, they might add some hot dishes like bacon and eggs or steak pie. Tea is customarily served from fancy silver teapots into beautiful delicate bone china cups. Milk and lemon are traditionally served for those who may enjoy enhancing their tea.

There are a few tips to keep in mind. First, if you are using any decorations, keep them simple and in soft colorful tones. Second, if you are using flat dishes for serving your snacks, make sure you do not mix the sandwiches with the sweets, and don't forget to cut the crusts off the sandwiches. If you are serving with tiered dishes, place the cakes on top, then the scones, then the finger sandwiches.

> How to Brew Tea

1. Using a pot or tea kettle on the stove, heat the water to just boiling.

2. Add tea bags to your teapot, or loose tea. You'll need approximately 1 bag (or 1 tablespoon) per cup of tea.

3. Pour hot water over tea; fill your teapot.

4. Let steep 3-6 minutes, depending on the kind of tea and your preferences.

5. If you used tea bags, remove them.

6. If you used loose tea, let it settle to the bottom of the teapot.

7. Pour tea into cups and serve.

8. Add sugar cubes, milk or lemon slices if you like.

9. Drink and enjoy.

Simple. Classic. Parties.

> Tea Brewing Temperature Guide

The best brewing temperature for teas has been a question to many. The bottom line is this: it's a matter of personal choice and the manner in which you brew. Most teas will make you a respectable cup of tea if you steep them in boiling water. However, you may find that your finer teas will do better at a lower temperature. As an example, green and white teas, which are considered more delicate and flavorful, do better in slightly cooler water.

Please keep in mind that these steeping times are only approximate, and you should adjust them according to your own personal tea enjoyment.

BLACK TEA	Black is the most robust of the tea family and can be brewed in truly boiling water. It usually should be steeped for 4-6 minutes.
GREEN TEA	Green teas are more delicate and need to be treated accordingly. The water temperature should be around 150-160°F, and it should be steeped for only 2-4 minutes.
OOLONG TEA	Oolong tea falls between green and black. The best temperature is usually around 190°F. It should be steeped longer than black tea, around 5-8 minutes.
ROOIBOS TEA	This red herbal tea is from South Africa and is very hardy. It should be prepared with fully boiling water, as with black tea.
WHITE TEA	This is another delicate tea that needs to be treated gently. The water can be a little warmer than what you use for green tea, about 180°F. Let it steep longer, at least 4-6 minutes.
MOST HERBAL TEAS	Considering the countless choices of herbs that can be used for herbal tea blends, it's impossible to offer any steeping or temperature guidelines that would be truly accurate. A good rule of thumb would be that most herbs can be brewed in boiling water and steeped for about 5 minutes. The best thing to do would be to try different times and see what gives you the flavor you want.

Not everybody has a thermometer, and if you don't want to buy one, you can usually figure out the water temperature by observing the bubbles. Small bubbles will float to the surface of the water at 160-170°F, and you'll see strings of bubbles from the bottom of the kettle at 180-190°F. Next comes a full rolling boil.

The best temperature for brewing tea is a matter of personal choice and the manner in which you brew.

Simple. Classic. Parties.

> Loose Tea versus Tea Bags

You may ask yourself, what's the difference between bagged teas and loose teas? The answer is the size of the leaves. That's what influences the finished cup of tea. The wonderful flavors of tea come from the chemicals and essential oils that are in the tea leaves. If the leaves break up and the oils evaporate, you'll get a boring cup of tea. In general, loose teas are made up of whole leaves or large pieces. However, tea bags are normally filled with what's called "fannings," which are tiny pieces of broken leaves.

Besides the leaf size, there is also the space factor to consider. It is important for tea leaves to have enough space to swell, expand and unfurl, and you must have good water circulation around the leaves. Unfortunately, in tea bags, the leaves don't have that. They're squished in a little bag.

On some tea bag boxes, you will see the words "Orange Pekoe." This does not refer to the flavor or kind of tea; rather, it refers to a grade of tea. It is actually considered by many to be a good grade, but not the greatest. Leaf size determines the grade. To some, Orange Pekoe is not considered a true whole leaf tea.

Even if you prefer a simple cup of tea, expand your tea horizons and experiment with some loose tea. Although there is a very wide variety of teas in bags, there are even more choices in loose tea. Try something different.

Simple. Classic. Parties.

> Children's Tea Party

Can you remember your first tea set? My set was made of china; it was white and had little flowers all over it. It had a teapot with tiny cups and saucers. Being given this beautiful tea set was the catalyst for throwing my first tea party with a teddy bear, my favorite dolls, and my dog as my guests. The scene was simple: a table, two chairs, a tea set, and my imagination. Let's not forget a plate of cookies and my teapot filled with water.

I shared my very first cups of "tea" along with homemade chocolate chip cookies with my mother. Once in a while my brother, Steven, would try to sneak in for the cookies, but we wouldn't let him stay — of course not. He was a boy!

There is nothing more important than creating memories with your children. The first step to get you started in creating this particular memory is to decide what kind of tea party you want to have. Do you want to keep it simple, or do you want to have a theme and decorate? The good news is you can pick a theme from anywhere. Once you've done that, before you go to the store, check to see if you have any supplies on hand that you can use to help create and develop your theme. Get a pad of paper and write down the things you would like and what you will need. If you're going all out, a tea party can have five elements: costumes, crafts and activities, decorations, recipes, teas and juices. Keep in mind that all of these elements can be designed based on you and your child's likes and creativity.

If you will be offering teas to the children, be cautious of what you select. It's obvious not a good idea to give children caffeinated teas, so choose herbal teas. When you're in the tea section at the market, know that herbal tea packages usually list their actual ingredients, such as mango, apple, peach or lemon. It's best not to buy herbal teas just by their name; check the ingredients and look for the flavor you want. If you do not want to offer tea because you are not comfortable with it, that's perfectly fine. Substitute with some tasty juices.

TEA TREATS: When you want to serve a traditional tea, even to children, you must plan the menu. The first thing on the list should be tea sandwiches. They are small, about two to three bites each, and perfect for children. Of course, you should also serve a variety of yummy cookies and mini cupcakes. You can serve your treats on traditional tiered trays so you can teach the girls the proper way to help themselves at a tea, from the bottom up. Or, if you don't have tiered trays, regular dinner plates will do as serving dishes.

Regardless of what you serve, or what your theme may be, children's tea parties must have bright colors, delicious simple food and lots of fun. Lastly, and probably the most important, children (or should I say princesses) like to be part of everything, so get your little princess involved right from the beginning planning stages. If she likes to cook, ask her to join you in the kitchen. You can even have a little cup of tea while you work. All of this is a wonderful opportunity for you to create new memories.

Simple. Classic. Parties.

> Menu Ideas

TEA SANDWICHES	Peanut butter and jelly
	Cream cheese and jelly
	Egg, tuna or chicken salad
TEA SWEETS	Fruit-flavored scones
	Mini cupcakes
	Assorted cookies
	Mini doughnuts
	Brownies
REGULAR DRINKS	Flavored cold tea — mango, raspberry
	Hot chocolate
	Hot tea
	Juices — apple, grape
	Lemonade
	Limeade
	Pink lemonade
SPECIALTY DRINKS	"Bubbly Treat" — Pour chilled sparkling apple cider or white grape juice into plastic flutes and add any of the following: a fresh strawberry, pureed fresh or canned peaches, some fresh-squeezed orange juice
	"Smoothies" — Set out ice, apple juice, yogurt, bananas, berries and sliced peaches with a blender and let kids create (with supervision) their own drink
	"Special Hot Chocolate" — Embellish this favorite with any of the following: marshmallows and/or whipped cream; cinnamon and vanilla; an orange peel garnish; or chopped peppermint candies and a candy cane swizzle stick

Simple. Classic. Parties.

China

According to legend, the Chinese emperor Shen Nung discovered tea more than 5,000 years ago. He was boiling his drinking water when a few leaves fell in, and he so enjoyed the resulting brew that he ordered tea bushes be planted around his palace. And so the custom of steeping tea leaves in boiling water became firmly entrenched in China's culture.

For many years, through to the fifth century A.D., tea was mainly used for medicinal purposes in China. After that time, however, it also became popular as a gift within the upper classes, and people served and drank tea at social events and in private homes. The Chinese tea ceremony was developed around this time, as well, and the custom soon spread to Japan.

Japan

Tea first came to Japan in the seventh or eighth century after a Buddhist monk who had been studying in China brought home green tea. For many years after, tea was used mainly in Buddhist monasteries, for medicinal purposes and as a meditation aid. Then, in 1191 A.D., a Buddhist monk brought matcha, a powdered green tea, to Japan from China, and soon the Japanese tea ceremony, the ritual used to prepare matcha tea, developed.

In the 18th century, tea producers created a new and more practical means of producing green tea, making the drink more accessible to everyone; in the 19th century, tea production was automated, and it became even more widely available. Green tea remains a staple of the Japanese diet today, and practitioners of the Japanese tea ceremony perform the ritual all over the world.

tea traditions in

France

France's King Louis XIV was one of the first in his country to drink tea, in the 17th century. He took tea for his health, to help with his gout and to fend off heart problems. But after the French Revolution, tea fell out of favor, as it was associated with aristocracy. Eventually, its popularity returned, and now, in modern-day France, tea-drinkers choose from a wide variety of tea blends. They pair them with French pastries, many times in the elegant tea salons that flourish throughout the country.

England

Though the United Kingdom and Ireland now consume more tea than any other country besides China, the drink did not come to Europe through England. Instead, it first appeared in Holland or Portugal, brought home via the Far East sea trade routes. Tea didn't reach England until the mid-1600s, and even then, it wasn't that popular. It took until the mid-1700s to catch on. But by the mid-1800s, England had become one of the biggest importers of tea. The high demand made the price quite high, though, and only the wealthy could afford it.

However, as India started to produce more tea in the late 1800s, the price got lower, and tea became a regular part of a normal British day. Today, most tea drinkers in England prefer stronger black tea varieties like Earl Grey and English Breakfast.

India

Today, India produces more tea than any other country in the world. But the nation's tea industry only developed in the 19th century because England could no longer rely on China to fulfill its demand for tea. Tea plants are indigenous to India, but the drink did not become a part of the Indian diet until after the British started producing tea there around 1850.

India is well known for its Darjeeling tea, known as the "Champagne of teas," which is grown high in the Himalayas, as well as its Assam teas, which are stronger black teas. In India, black tea is often consumed as chai: tea blended with spices and served with milk.

other Countries

Russia

Tea first appeared in Russia in the 1600s, when Chinese rulers gave crates of tea leaves to Russian tsars as gifts. Within a few decades, a tea trade between the two countries had been established, but the price of the delicacy was so high that only the wealthy could afford it. By the late 1700s, however, enough tea was being imported that middle and lower class Russians could afford it, and it grew in popularity. In Russia, tea is traditionally made in a samovar, a combination of water heater and teapot, and served in glassware encased in metallic tea-glass holders.

entertaining your way

chapter six

When we have family and/or friends over, we obviously want to put our best foot forward, we might think that we have to use our fancy china, cook a gourmet meal, and even possibly have an elaborate centerpiece on the table. What I have realized over many years of entertaining is that your basics such as white plates and bowls, clear glasses, always work. These contemporary classics are simple yet adaptable enough to work for virtually any occasion, whether you are having an everyday dinner, a stylish cocktail party, or a fabulous holiday gathering. Unlike decorative bone china that you might save only for formal dinners, or patterned plates that you would use on a daily basis, white china and clear glassware can be easily dressed up or down or combined with any and all colors. If it's an issue for you, another advantage is that it can save you some money in the long run, as white pottery and clear glassware are available from a countless array of retailers for very reasonable prices. My point is you don't have to set a fancy table. You have choices, do what works for you. Do what you feel like doing.

When you select your décor and place setting for your table, keep in mind that it will help set the tone for your party. Remember that it's not what everything costs that's important, but how much thought you put into it. The table will reflect who you are. So, don't take your table setting too seriously. Be creative and have fun with it.

table components

> Dinnerware

When it comes to dishes, the choices are endless. They can range from bone china to earthware, to porcelain, to pottery and stoneware. The only limitations are your budget and how many stores you want to go to if you don't already have the style you want at home. As I say about entertaining, there are no set rules here. It's a matter of taste and what you already have. The key is to use pieces that harmonize with each other. For example, I wouldn't recommend that you use stoneware with bone china. It's always appropriate to use basic white dinnerware and that accent your table with colorful pieces. This works for almost all gatherings. If you don't have a full set, try to serve each course on matching plates. Once you know how many people are coming, make sure you inventory your plates so you know how many you have and whether you need to get more.

> Glassware

Some people believe that all your glasses have to match. Not so. They should just be comparable in quality and style. Clear, simply designed glassware always works. If you have colored glasses, you can certainly accent with them. However; when it comes to the stemware, colored glass can conflict with the color of the wine. If you have crystal, a party is the time to use it. The glow from crystal can light up a table.

Before you can actually decide on the types of glassware that you will need, you must first decide what wines and drinks you would like to serve your guests. For dinner, if you would like to serve a wine with each course, then make sure you have the right number of glasses for each person. The reality is, any wine can be served in any glass, but if you already have some, or if you want to go buy some, good wineglasses are particularly designed to not only enhance a wine's character, but also to add to your pleasure. You will notice that a wine glass bowl is designed to help increase the flavor and bouquet. The stem is there as a holding tool, so you keep your hand off the bowl and thereby don't change the temperature of the wine.

If you want to buy stemware, keep your eye out for thin-walled glasses that feel sturdy in your hand. Wineglasses are available in all kinds of sizes and shapes. But all one really needs are the basics: flutes, dessert wine, red wine, and white wine.

FLUTES are best to serve champagne and other sparkling wines in. Their tall, thin shape decreases the wine's surface area, keeping the bubbles from dissolving and enhancing their fizz.

DESSERT WINE OR PORT GLASSES are the shape of wineglasses, but they are much smaller because such high-alcohol and enriched wines are served in small portions.

WHITE-WINE GLASSES can be tulip-shaped, with a tapered top. When buying them, look for a large bowl with plenty of room to gently swirl the wine and enjoy its aromatic bouquet. If you are in the beginning stages of your wineglass collection, you can absolutely start with these because they can be used for anything.

RED-WINE GLASSES look like white wine glasses, but bigger. Burgundy glasses are bubble-shaped, with a fuller bowl designed to draw out the complexity of the wine and maximize its aromas. They are perfect for your lighter reds with more subtle aromas, such as Pinot Noir. These same glasses can also be used to enjoy sophisticated white Burgundies. The largest Bordeaux glass has straight sides that allow more air to be fused into the wine, and they're best matched with the more full-bodied wines, such as Cabernet Sauvignon.

> Flatware

When you're coordinating your flatware, you just have to make sure it's all of the same quality and style, not that it all matches. To start, a basic set of silver-toned flatware is all you need. If you like that old-fashioned elegant style, there's nothing quite like sterling silver. The bad news is that it does require a good amount of maintenance, because you have to polish it. As beautiful as it looks when you're done, it's very time-consuming. That's why most people who have it only bring it out for special occasions. Nowadays, I don't think that many people even buy it like they did years ago. Silver plate is one step below sterling. It's less expensive but still requires some special care. Then there's good quality stainless steel. This is probably the most popular style in most homes and can be used for almost all occasions. What's more, you can throw it in the dishwasher. If you don't have flatware and you want to buy some, go to the store and pick up a couple of different pieces in your hand, one at a time, and see how they feel. Is it light and comfortable or heavy and awkward? Then make your decision.

> Serving Pieces

Design can be about taking something out of its "expected" place and using it in unexpected ways. We've seen this thinking in high fashion design many times, but it can also work at your table, with serving pieces. Think outside of the box, review these ideas, and let them help to stir your creative senses to create your own ideas.

SMALL TONGS	These were originally created for smaller item like ice or olives. Try them also for sliced meats, some lighter vegetables, like green beans or asparagus, and your bite size hors d'oeuvres.
SOUP LADLES	Use for gravy boats, dessert sauces and toppings. Your bigger ladles are for soups or punches.
PIE SERVERS	A great tool for small flat appetizers, as well as sliced vegetables.
LITTLE RELISH FORKS	Perfect for your smaller appetizers like shrimp, smoked salmon and chunks of fresh fruit.
DEMITASSE SPOONS	Great for condiments or caviar.
SMALL WOODEN SCOOPS	Make it easy to help yourself to very small items such as candies, cocktail onions, nuts or olives.
BUTTER SPREADERS	The ideal tool for all kinds of soft cheeses, flavorful spreads, mousses, or pates.

Simple. Classic. Parties.

1. **Napkin**

2. **Salad Fork**

3. **Dinner Fork**

4. **Dessert Fork & Coffee Spoon**

5. **Bread & Butter Plate with Spreader**

6. **Dinner Plate**

7. **Dinner Knife**

8. **Teaspoon**

9. **Teaspoon**

10. **Soup Spoon**

11. **Cocktail Fork**

12. **Water Glass**

13. **Red Wine Glass**

14. **White Wine Glass**

15. **Coffee Cup & Saucer**

dinner party

4

6

7   8   9   10   11

12

13

14

15

table setting

> Linens

Tablecloths and napkins come in all colors and patterns. But for a basic set, you could go with high-quality cotton or linen in the white or cream tones. These colors go with everything and and all settings. Don't feel you have to run out and buy a tablecloth for each set of dishes you have.

The process of buying a tablecloth is really quite simple. First you measure your table, allowing about 18-inches for the overhang. You want to make sure that the overhang isn't so long that it will interfere with your dinner guests' legs.

Some people save their tablecloths for fancier occasions, but they can be used for any occasion. Even if you're having a very casual affair, it's a nice change from using placemats.

If your tablecloth has some wrinkles that you just can't iron out, try to align the wrinkles with the center and sides of your table. Sometimes this helps them to not be so noticeable.

If you want to try something a little different, try a table runner. These are long, thin strips of fabric that go down the center of your table. The runner could even be a bright color to add a little something extra to your table. The runner is usually wide enough to put your serving dishes on, but it means your plates have to go on the table itself, or you have to use placemats. Or, you could also use a runner on either side so it looks like you have three strips. In any case, be creative, try different things, then do what you like best.

When it comes choosing a cloth napkin, something plain is always appropriate. If you have napkins that are monogrammed, by all means use them. To fold them, make sure that the monogram is on the lower left hand corner or the center of the bottom of the napkin. As to where to place the napkin, you have choices; it could go on the left under the forks, to the left of the forks, or on the top of the plate. My favorite is to grab the middle of the napkin with two fingers, shake it, fold the bottom third up and stick it in a glass so it looks like a flower.

That all being said, most people today just like to put it under the forks, especially when space is an issue. You could also fold or roll the napkin and put it in a napkin ring. Then you can either place it to the left of the plate, across the plate or right above the plate. The cloth itself doesn't have to match for informal affairs, it only has to blend. However, for formal affairs, the linens should all match.

Here's a little tip: A napkin doesn't have to be a napkin; it can be almost any cloth at all. Depending on your meal, be creative. If you're serving a messy barbecue, use a dish towel (along with a moist towel to clean up). For something light like hot dogs, use a bandana. You can always use linen, or a finger towel or a terry cloth towel. Here are a few suggestions as to how you can fold your napkin. It doesn't have to be square:

Draped by grabbing it in the middle and laying it on the plate.

Knotted in the middle and laid across the plate.

Pulled through a napkin ring; for a brunch you could use a plain bagel.

Rolled up and tied with ribbon or thin rope.

Tied around a small bouquet of flowers or a single large flower.

Wrapped like cones around buffet flatware and arranged on a tray or in a basket.

> Decorative Elements

It's always nice to have a variety of small vases that are different sizes and colors. They are ideal for decorating your table. Sometimes a vase is so delicate you need something to weight it down so it doesn't fall over. Most of the time I use clear round tiny pieces of glass that you can buy in a hardware store or nursery. If your vase is large, you can use rocks from your garden or even small pieces of fruit like lemons or limes. When picking your vases, be creative and don't just stick to the traditional items. Almost anything can be used as a vase, even a bar glass.

CENTERPIECES can be a cheerful and festive way to go. Just don't get too wild with the design. It's important for conversation that the centerpiece is never so high that it blocks the line of vision of your guests. Low and simple is always appropriate. Over the last few years, edible centerpieces have become very popular. A decorative bowl or basket, whatever you have, is a wonderful vehicle for fresh fruit such as apples, oranges, pears, or whatever is in season.

FLOWERS are the most traditional preference for a centerpiece. It's important to stay away from flowers with a strong scent, not just because you may have a guest with allergy issues, but also because you don't want them to fight with the aromas of your delicious food. Be careful that none of your flowers or greenery are so long that they reach over toward any of your guests' plates. You don't want to have a leaf or petal in your wine glass. You can either buy the flowers already in a vase, or you can buy a bunch and arrange them yourself. If you choose to do it yourself, first you cut the stems on the diagonal so they absorb water better. Then you want to strip away the leaves that would be below the water line. It will make it look cleaner and more open.Try not to put the flowers in any direct sun, as they won't stay fresh.

SATELLITES are small groups of flowers, or other bright and fun items, that can be put around the social area to design various points of interest that help to tie all the décor together. You can be as creative as you want in this area, too. You can put things together in a little bunch, line them up down a table, or put them across a fireplace.

CANDLES come in all kinds of sizes, colors and shapes. But for a dinner table, they should either be short, like votives, or tall enough so they don't interfere in anyone's line of sight. If you go with the short ones, make sure they are low enough so that if your guests reach across the table over the candle, they don't burn themselves. If you choose tall candles, make sure that they are very secure in their holders, as they can fall over, especially if someone or something accidentally brushes against it. In terms of colors, you can't go wrong with white or off-white, and they should be unscented and dripless. Normally candles aren't used at daytime events, but you certainly could use them as decoration on your table, unlit.

> Setting the Table

Before you can just start setting the table, you have to ask yourself, will all my guests fit comfortably? A good rule of thumb is to plan for about 2 feet of space starting from the center of one plate to the center of the next plate. This is especially important for your formal dinners.

Whether your gathering is formal or casual, you do not have to be a professional designer to create and develop a beautiful warm and inviting table. If you are feeling some uncertainty as to what to do, keep it simple. Start with white or off-white, then accent the table with a little color. Be careful not to go over the top. Let your glassware and flatware provide the oomph.

Here are some guidelines for you to consider:

1. For small groups, you can use round tables: 48 inches for six people, 54 inches for eight.

2. A 60-inch round is not conducive to conversation, so for 10 or more people, narrow rectangular tables are better.

3. Make sure you iron the tablecloth completely. Pay extra attention to the creases from where the cloth was folded. Store your tablecloth either lying flat in a shelf or drawer, or hang it on a special hanger in a closet that doesn't get much use. First iron the napkins flat, being careful to get into the corners. You can then fold them the way you want and lightly iron them again, or just leave them as is and put them on the table.

4. The knives and spoons go to the right of the plate, with the sharp side of the knife facing in, and the forks go to the left. Silverware that is used first go the farthest from the plate. If you're having a formal dinner, you can put a dessert fork and teaspoon on the table above the dinner plate. Some hosts even put them face down so they don't get dirty during the course of the meal.

5. The glasses go by the tip of the knife. The wineglass is set to the right of the water glass.

6. If you are using place cards, they go on the plate or on the table, centered at the top of your guests' plates. You can use plain white or decorative cardboard cards folded in half with the person's name, but you can also try something creative, like a name card glued to a small stick that's stuck into a small piece of fruit or vegetable, or a small vase with a flower in it, name card taped to the outside, or a small antique picture frame with the person's name in it.

7. Pick up your flowers the day before. Sometimes they need a little extra time to open.

8. When possible, try to make the light that's coming from the table brighter than the above lights. It will keep your guests eye refocusing towards the center.

9. Make sure your candles are not blocking anyone's view.

10. Once you have finished setting the table, sit down at one end and look across the table. Is anything blocking your vision? If so, make the necessary adjustments. If not, you're ready to go.

Simple. Classic. Parties.

> The Informal Table

Nothing sets the tone for your menu like your setting. A casual table implies a casual menu.

Choose a plain tablecloth or fun place mats and use simple napkins. Your dishes, flatware and glassware that you use every day will work just fine. If you feel like it, bring in a couple of special pieces.

At each guest's place, you can have a napkin either to the left of the plate with its folded edge facing the plate, or on top of the plate. Position the flatware in the order in which it will be needed, going from the farthest point coming in. You can either put your flatware on the napkin itself, or you can put it to the right, depending on your space. If you are putting it to the right, place a salad fork down first, and then the larger dinner fork. On the right side of the plate, place your dinner knife with the blade facing inward. Next place a single teaspoon, to balance your standard setting, or double teaspoons, one for the meal and one for dessert. If you are also serving soup, then place your soup spoon after your teaspoons.

I always put the glassware down last. It's just too easy to accidently hit a glass as you're reaching over the table to put dishes down. The first glass would be your water glass, and it goes at the tip of your dinner knife; next to it goes a wine glass. If you are serving multiple wines, have multiple glasses. It is not necessary to put out bread knives and plates for an informal meal. It's perfectly acceptable for your guests to put their bread directly on their dinner plate. For the casual occasion, be creative and think outside the box.

Here are just a few ways to add a little interest to your table:

1. Try going to estate or garage sales. Look out for unusual plates to use as serving plates. Use them as chargers — plates that go under your first-course plate.

2. Be artistic and mix and match your china and flatware. Your place settings or patterns can be different. This is an ideal solution when you don't have enough of one pattern.

3. Be creative with your table coverings, large and small. Think outside the traditional ways. Go to a local fabric store and see what they have that's interesting and colorful, or check your linen closet for sheets or light quilts.

4. Play around with layers of colors and textures. Take out one of your light-colored tablecloths and lay a runner down the center that's a completely different color.

5. Whatever you do, don't forget the candles. As I keep saying, be creative and try the unexpected. Consider using unusual shaped glass containers, bar glasses, a grouping of votives on a bright and colorful plate, or floating candles. These are some of my personal favorites. You put them in a shallow bowl with some water, and you just let them float.

Add interest to an informal table: mix and match china and flatware patterns, playing with different colors and textures.

> The Formal Table

A winning formal table setting is more about the sharing of a special occasion than about the setting of the table. It's the perfect time to bring out the good stuff ⊠ the best china, linen, flatware and glassware you have. The key to the table is warmth and class, not cold and flash. The table should say, "Welcome, we're glad you're here."

The formal meal always calls for each guest to have his or her own plate. Silver and gold chargers look sophisticated as plate holders. The charger stays on the table through the first course, like a salad or soup. When the salad and/or soup are cleared from the table, the charger goes, too. Then your entrée is served.

There are several similarities between the formal and informal table when it comes to the napkins and flatware. They both have the napkin to the left with the folded side facing the plate, or it can also be centered on the plate in a special folded way. Some hosts put the napkin between the charger and the plate for a little more unusual look.

As usual, if you want your forks to the right of the napkin, make sure you have them positioned with the first fork needed placed the farthest from the plate. For example, if you are serving a salad, put the salad fork to the left of the dinner fork. If you want to bring it up a notch, keep everyone's salad fork in the refrigerator. Then, after everyone is seated, take the forks out, place them inside a folded napkin, then put them on a pretty plate and go from guest to guest, asking them to take a fork.

As usual, your dinner knife will go to the right of the plate, with its blade facing inward. Lay out your dessert utensils at this time, too. Place the fork down with the handle to the left and the spoon with the handle to the right. If your table isn't big enough to hold these items comfortably, that's OK. You can bring them out with the dessert. You don't want the table to look crowded.

To continue with the formal look, place a small bread and butter plate just left of the forks. Make sure the knife is laid on the upper rim of the plate with the handle to the right and the sharp edge facing in. Perhaps the main difference between a formal and informal table is the bread plate.

As you set your table, regardless of the table setting, always have a dish towel on hand to wipe down the silverware if needed. Don't assume because they haven't been used or just came from the dishwasher that they're clean.

All of the glassware or stemware that will be needed for the meal should be set at each guest's plate. It should be positioned in a diagonal line above the dinner knife in order of enjoyment, from the closest to the farthest. As a guideline, a white wine is usually served with the first course, so place it just above the tip of the knife. Next, you have the larger red wine glass, which is typically used with the entrée. Place this glass diagonally up and to the left of the first glass. Last, you will have a large goblet for water. Place this one diagonally up and to the left of the last glass. Depending on the order and types of wines offered, the order I've recommended can change. But you always have the water glass at the leftmost position.

It's always nice if you have a lot of small sets of salt and pepper shakers. It's a nice touch to have a set for every two to four guests. Make sure your pepper grinders are filled with fresh whole peppercorns, not ground.

> The Buffet

A buffet should have the look and feel of welcome and plenty. The food should smell delicious and should be colorful and beautifully plated. To accomplish this, you must start off with the right table. It shouldn't be too big or it will look like you don't have enough food, and it shouldn't be too small because you don't want everything to be crowded and unappealing. Once you have your table(s) out, do a dry run and place your serving pieces on the table to see how it looks. That is the time to move things around, before they're loaded with food. I would recommend that you even draw yourself a placement plan.

If you have room, pull the food table out away from the wall so there's enough room for your guests to walk by both sides. For larger buffets, if you can, divide each dish by two and create a mirrored effect down both sides of the table. It definitely helps to keep the crowd moving.

It's important to cover the buffet table with a tablecloth. Once you have established the flow of traffic, set the plates at one end and the napkins and flatware at the other end. This way, your guests won't have to worry about napkins and utensils while they are helping themselves. To make serving easier, roll the silverware up in the napkin so when they pick it up they have everything at one time. If you are having a formal affair, set your silverware and napkins at the eating tables.

It's important to have your food positioned in the order in which your guests will be enjoying them: first course/salad, main course, side dishes, and so on. Make sure that you have the proper serving pieces for each dish you are serving. If your guests will be coming down both sides of the table, make sure you have two of everything in each dish. Alternately, you can put cold dishes before hot ones and carved meats toward the end of the buffet. If you are having a carving dish, do not let your guests carve for themselves. Not only does this keep the flow going, but you also won't have to worry about your guests either cutting themselves or getting something on their clothes. This kind of area is traditionally called a carving station, and it's always a nice touch for a special occasion. Remember that people like to know what they're eating. On plain white place cards, write out the names of each item, and place them in front of the appropriate dishes.

If you have a big room or a separate table, you can have your desserts out at the beginning. If not, once the meal has been served and people are done taking food, not necessarily eating, you can clean away the entrée dishes and bring out your desserts. If your tablecloth is a mess, replace it with a fresh one.

You'll also need separate table for drinks. This should be located away from the main buffet to help avoid traffic jams. If you have a lot of extra space, set up two drink areas, one for alcohol and one for non-alcohol.

When positioning your food on your buffet table, it's always nice to have your dishes at different levels. It gives your table more interest, and sometimes it can even give you more room. To raise your dishes, you can use things like blocks or bricks, or you can place dishes on boxes. If you do something like this make sure you put the risers under the tablecloth. You can also use taller dishes that have pedestals or are footed.

Now that you have made all the decisions on what goes where and how, it's time to think about decorating. The first thing that always comes to mind is a centerpiece. That's a great idea, as long as it doesn't impede with the food. Flowers with a delicate scent are always a wonderful idea. However, make sure the flowers you select don't drop pedals or anything else. Candles are also a good idea but you must be careful with their placement because they can be easily knocked over. If your buffet is going to only have one side open to your guests, place your centerpiece either in the middle, against the wall, or at one of the ends. If you are offering a buffet that will be open on both sides, place your centerpiece in the middle. If you have extra room, you can place low, well-balanced vases along the table.

> The Buffet (CONTINUED)

As your guests are helping themselves and enjoying their food, keep an eye on the buffet table. You don't want to have to replenish or replace a platter when it's already empty, because your guests will have to wait for you to return with the full dish. If you have hired someone to help you, make sure they know when you want them to switch out platters. Don't assume they are going to know your wishes. And, make sure that you have those extra platters already set to go in the kitchen.

Keeping buffet food at a warm temperature can be a real task. If you have hot plates or chafing dishes, or know someone who does, use them. You can also heat oversized tiles in the oven and place them under the serving platter on an insulating material. You can also heat large ceramic or terracotta tiles in a 250 degree oven until they are hot, which will be about 15 to 20 minutes. Make sure you use a very heavy pot holder when you take them out. Put the tiles on the insulating material just before you are ready to bring out the food. It is imperative that you cover the buffet surface with a thick heat-resistant material, or fold a thick tablecloth several times to form a safe area for the tiles. This will protect the table and help the food keep warm. Place the warmed platters of food on the top of the hot tiles very carefully, and let your guests know that the tiles under the platters are hot. You might even want to make a little sign to put next to the platters that says "Hot Platter." You know your guests; use your judgment.

> Final Tips for Your Table

Be creative; be colorful. If you're in the mood, mix and match. What you have just read constitutes nothing more than my own ideas and suggestions. Make your table be "you," mixed with whatever the occasion or holiday may be.

"Toda" or Thank You

Writing a book was not something that I had thought about doing for a long time. It all came about one evening when we were at a friend's house for dinner and she said, *"why don't you write a book about what you do best."* So, thank you to Pam, who had the idea. When I finished the first draft I thought I better find a publisher. So, I went online and started researching publishers. They were everywhere, in every city and every state. As I found someone that was interesting, I would call and interview them on the phone. But, I wasn't clicking with anyone. Then I found Victoria Bailey of Desert Springs Publishing. We clicked immediately. We met, we talked and that was it. So thank you to Victoria, for being my Publisher, my friend, and for helping me to learn Mah Jong.

Now, every book needs a fabulous graphic designer and art director. Lucky for me, Victoria introduced me to Thomas Granade. Thomas and I hit it off from day one also. When you meet the right people you know it immediately. Thomas is extremely talented and hard working. He also doesn't settle. It has to be right. So thank you to Thomas, for being my designer, my friend, teaching me to pick out a photo with an art director's eye and for teaching me how to play Scrabble, the right way, on my iPad.

Every book also needs an editor. I have been very lucky because I have had two. In the beginning, Karen Oppenheim was with us. Thank you to Karen for not only being with us when everything first started, but for being my friend, too. As time went on, we were lucky to have Robin Jones join our team. Thank you to Robin for being there when we needed her, even when it was at a moment's notice.